TEACHER'S PET PUBLICATIONS

PUZZLE PACK
for
The Canterbury Tales
based on the tales by
Geoffrey Chaucer

Written by
William T. Collins

© 2005 Teacher's Pet Publications
All Rights Reserved

The materials in this packet are copyrighted
by Teacher's Pet Publications, Inc.

These pages may be duplicated by the purchaser
for use in the purchaser's own classroom.

Copying any of these materials and distributing them
for any other purpose is a violation of the copyright laws.

© 2005 Teacher's Pet Publications, Inc.
www.tpet.com

INTRODUCTION
If you already own the LitPlan for this title, this Puzzle Pack will refresh your Unit Resource Materials and Vocabulary Resource Materials sections plus give you additional materials you can substitute into the tests. If you do not already have a complete LitPlan, these pages will give you some supplemental materials to use with your own plan. There are two main groups of materials: one set for unit words (such as characters' names, symbols, places, etc.) and one set for vocabulary words associated with the book.

WORD LIST
There is a word list for both the unit words and the vocabulary words. These lists show you which words are being used in the materials and the clues or definitions being used for those words. You may want to give students a word list with clues/definitions to help them, or you may want students to only have a word list (without clues/definitions) if you want them to work a little harder. Both are available for duplication. The word lists can also be your "calling key" for the bingo games.

FILL IN THE BLANK AND MATCHING
There are 4 each of the fill in the blank and matching worksheets for both the unit and vocabulary words. These pages can be used either as extra worksheets for students or as objective parts of a unit test. They can be done individually if students need extra help or as a whole class activity to review the material covered.

MAGIC SQUARES
The magic squares not only reinforce the material covered but also work on reasoning and math skills. Many teachers have told us that their students really enjoy doing these!

WORD SEARCH PUZZLES
The word search words go in all directions, as indicated on your answer keys. Two of the word search puzzles have the clues listed rather than the words. This makes the puzzle a little more difficult, but it reinforces the material better. Two word search puzzles have words only for students who find the clue puzzles too difficult.

CROSSWORD PUZZLES
Both unit and vocabulary word sections have 4 crossword puzzles.

BINGO CARDS
There are 32 individual bingo cards for the unit words and 32 individual bingo cards for the vocabulary words. You can use your word list as a "call list," calling the words at random and marking them off of your list as you go, or you could use the flash cards by cutting them apart and drawing the words at random from a hat (or box or whatever). To make a better review, you might ask for the definition and spelling of each word as you call it out–or you could call out the definitions and have students tell you the words they need to look for on the puzzle.

JUGGLE LETTERS
The vocabulary juggle letter game is intended to help students learn the spellings of the words. One sheet has the definitions listed on it as an extra help for students who need it or to reinforce the definitions if you choose to do so.

FLASH CARDS
We've included a set of vocabulary flash cards you can duplicate, cut, and fold for your students. Some teachers make a few sets for general use by the class; others make a set for each student. Some teachers duplicate them for each student and have the students cut & fold their own. You can cut out just the words and put them in a hat, have each student pick out one word and write the definition and a sentence for that word. Students then swap words and papers, with the next student adding a sentence of his own under the last one. You can have students swap as many times as you like. Each time the student will read the sentences written prior to his own and then add a sentence. You can cut out the words and definitions separately and play "I Have; Who Has?" Each student in the room draws a word and definition. The first student says, "I have (the name of the word). Who has the definition?" The student with the definition reads it then says, "I have (the name of the vocabulary word she has). Who has the definition?" The round continues until all words and definitions have been given.

The Canterbury Tales Unit Word List

No.	Word	Clue/Definition
1.	ABBEY	Place where they took the singing boy
2.	ABSALOM	Parish clerk who lusts after Alison
3.	ADULTERY	A young wife would help January from committing this sin
4.	ALAN	He slept with the miller's daughter
5.	ALISON	Carpenter's wife
6.	ALLEY	Place where the singing boy was attacked
7.	ARCITA	He won the contest for Emily's hand
8.	ARM	Carpenter broke his when he fell
9.	ARVERAGUS	Dorigen's husband
10.	AURELIUS	He tried to rid the coast of rocks for Dorigen
11.	BAILLY	Host
12.	BATH	Wife of ____
13.	BED	Where the merchant's wife was going to pay him back
14.	BOW	Arcita fell onto his and broke his breast
15.	BOY	He sang
16.	BRIBE	Money paid to the summoner to keep him from making an arrest
17.	CAKE	What the miller's wife made from the flour he took from A & J
18.	CHANTICLEER	The cock
19.	CHAUCER	Author
20.	CHILDREN	Walter brought the ____ back to Griselda
21.	CLERK	Loved to learn for the sake of learning
22.	CLOTHES	What the merchant's wife wanted to buy with her loan
23.	COOK	Had sores, master chef
24.	CURSE	The farmer didn't mean his, but the widow did
25.	DAMIAN	May meets him in a tree
26.	DEEDS	Griselda was beautiful in looks and ____
27.	DESIRE	The knight was sent to find the thing women most ____
28.	DIED	What happened to all three youths who found Death
29.	DORIGEN	She missed Arveragus
30.	DRUNK	Condition of the Miller as he told his tale
31.	EMILY	The queen's sister; two knights loved her
32.	EYES	Chanticleer closed his when he began to sing
33.	FAITH	The friar told Thomas he had to little of it
34.	FIEND	The yeoman's true identity
35.	FIVE	Number of husbands the Wife of Bath had
36.	FOX	It came to kill Chanticleer
37.	FRANCS	The loan amount: 100 ____
38.	FRANKLIN	Liked to eat, drink and be merry
39.	FRIAR	Aristocratic, takes bribes for easy penance
40.	GAS	Thomas's gift to the friar
41.	GOLD	It was under the tree
42.	GRISELDA	Marquis' new wife
43.	HEN	Pertelote, for example
44.	HONOR	Arveragus tried to help save Dorigen's
45.	IRE	Anger
46.	IRON	It branded Nicholas
47.	JOHN	He tricked the miller's wife into sleeping with him
48.	JOHNNY	The fifth husband of the Wife of Bath
49.	KISS	Alison agreed to do this to Absalom to make him go away
50.	KNIGHT	Had been in many battles, was a gentleman
51.	LOAN	The merchant's wife asked for one from Sir John

Copyrighted

The Canterbury Tales Unit Word List

No.	Word	Clue/Definition
52.	LOVE	The Wife of Bath married Johnny for this, not money
53.	MASTERY	What women most desire is ____ over husbands
54.	MAY	January's wife
55.	MERCHANT	Forked beard, good negotiator, always told his opinion
56.	MILLER	Football-player build, cheated customers, plays bagpipes
57.	MOLLY	Simpkin's daughter
58.	MONEY	The friar wanted the people to give ____ to pay for trentals
59.	MONK	Bald & fat, didn't like work
60.	NICHOLAS	Student boarder with Alison and the carpenter
61.	NUN	____'s Priest's Tale
62.	PALAMON	He married Emily after his cousin died
63.	PARDONER	Sells false relics, bulging eyes, long yellow hair
64.	PARSON	Christ-like, patient, giving, holy, virtuous
65.	PEAR	May claimed to desperately want one of this fruit
66.	PRAYER	The prologue to the Prioress's Tale is a ____
67.	PRIORESS	Dainty, pleasant, sensitive, medieval beauty
68.	PROLOGUE	The part that comes before the story
69.	REEVE	Old, thin, brought up the rear, good manager
70.	RELICS	Pardoner sells them as remedies
71.	SEA	Arveragus's castle was near the ____
72.	SEED	The monk took this from the boy's mouth
73.	SHAPES	Fiends take different ones to catch their prey
74.	SHIPMAN	Good navigator, didn't ride well, from Dartmouth
75.	SIMPKIN	The miller
76.	SMITH	From whom Absalom borrowed an iron
77.	SQUIRE	Son of the knight
78.	STAB	The older youths planned to do this to the youngest upon his return
79.	SUMMONER	Garland of flowers on head; insulted Friar
80.	TAIL	Place where the friars were hidden in hell
81.	THESEUS	Emily's brother-in-law; he captured two knights
82.	THROAT	The boy's was cut
83.	TOWER	Place where Theseus kept Arcita and Palamon
84.	TUBS	They were hung under the roof to serve as boats
85.	TWO	Number of years Arveragus was gone
86.	WHEEL	Squire's suggestion as to how to divide the gift
87.	YEAR	The knight had one ____ and one day to find an answer
88.	YEOMAN	Squire's servant
89.	YOUNG	The knight's old woman wife became ____ and beautiful

The Canterbury Tales Fill In The Blank 1

_____   1. He married Emily after his cousin died

_____   2. The yeoman's true identity

_____   3. It branded Nicholas

_____   4. Old, thin, brought up the rear, good manager

_____   5. It was under the tree

_____   6. She missed Arveragus

_____   7. Good navigator, didn't ride well, from Dartmouth

_____   8. Loved to learn for the sake of learning

_____   9. Bald & fat, didn't like work

_____   10. Liked to eat, drink and be merry

_____   11. The friar wanted the people to give ____ to pay for trentals

_____   12. The older youths planned to do this to the youngest upon his return

_____   13. The Wife of Bath married Johnny for this, not money

_____   14. The knight had one ____ and one day to find an answer

_____   15. He slept with the miller's daughter

_____   16. What the merchant's wife wanted to buy with her loan

_____   17. Wife of ____

_____   18. Football-player build, cheated customers, plays bagpipes

_____   19. Fiends take different ones to catch their prey

_____   20. Place where they took the singing boy

The Canterbury Tales Fill In The Blank 1 Answer Key

PALAMON	1. He married Emily after his cousin died
FIEND	2. The yeoman's true identity
IRON	3. It branded Nicholas
REEVE	4. Old, thin, brought up the rear, good manager
GOLD	5. It was under the tree
DORIGEN	6. She missed Arveragus
SHIPMAN	7. Good navigator, didn't ride well, from Dartmouth
CLERK	8. Loved to learn for the sake of learning
MONK	9. Bald & fat, didn't like work
FRANKLIN	10. Liked to eat, drink and be merry
MONEY	11. The friar wanted the people to give ____ to pay for trentals
STAB	12. The older youths planned to do this to the youngest upon his return
LOVE	13. The Wife of Bath married Johnny for this, not money
YEAR	14. The knight had one ____ and one day to find an answer
ALAN	15. He slept with the miller's daughter
CLOTHES	16. What the merchant's wife wanted to buy with her loan
BATH	17. Wife of ____
MILLER	18. Football-player build, cheated customers, plays bagpipes
SHAPES	19. Fiends take different ones to catch their prey
ABBEY	20. Place where they took the singing boy

The Canterbury Tales Fill In The Blank 2

_____
_____
_____
_____
_____
_____
_____
_____
_____
_____
_____
_____
_____
_____
_____
_____
_____
_____
_____
_____

1. Bald & fat, didn't like work
2. Arcita fell onto his and broke his breast
3. Griselda was beautiful in looks and ____
4. May claimed to desperately want one of this fruit
5. They were hung under the roof to serve as boats
6. What women most desire is ____ over husbands
7. The queen's sister; two knights loved her
8. The monk took this from the boy's mouth
9. Pardoner sells them as remedies
10. Fiends take different ones to catch their prey
11. Author
12. The miller
13. Liked to eat, drink and be merry
14. Wife of ____
15. The merchant's wife asked for one from Sir John
16. The knight had one ____ and one day to find an answer
17. Christ-like, patient, giving, holy, virtuous
18. A young wife would help January from committing this sin
19. He married Emily after his cousin died
20. The farmer didn't mean his, but the widow did

The Canterbury Tales Fill In The Blank 2 Answer Key

MONK	1. Bald & fat, didn't like work
BOW	2. Arcita fell onto his and broke his breast
DEEDS	3. Griselda was beautiful in looks and ____
PEAR	4. May claimed to desperately want one of this fruit
TUBS	5. They were hung under the roof to serve as boats
MASTERY	6. What women most desire is ____ over husbands
EMILY	7. The queen's sister; two knights loved her
SEED	8. The monk took this from the boy's mouth
RELICS	9. Pardoner sells them as remedies
SHAPES	10. Fiends take different ones to catch their prey
CHAUCER	11. Author
SIMPKIN	12. The miller
FRANKLIN	13. Liked to eat, drink and be merry
BATH	14. Wife of ____
LOAN	15. The merchant's wife asked for one from Sir John
YEAR	16. The knight had one ____ and one day to find an answer
PARSON	17. Christ-like, patient, giving, holy, virtuous
ADULTERY	18. A young wife would help January from committing this sin
PALAMON	19. He married Emily after his cousin died
CURSE	20. The farmer didn't mean his, but the widow did

The Canterbury Tales Fill In The Blank 3

_____ 1. Carpenter broke his when he fell

_____ 2. The cock

_____ 3. He sang

_____ 4. Anger

_____ 5. The fifth husband of the Wife of Bath

_____ 6. Squire's suggestion as to how to divide the gift

_____ 7. Christ-like, patient, giving, holy, virtuous

_____ 8. Carpenter's wife

_____ 9. Alison agreed to do this to Absalom to make him go away

_____ 10. Had been in many battles, was a gentleman

_____ 11. Number of husbands the Wife of Bath had

_____ 12. Bald & fat, didn't like work

_____ 13. Good navigator, didn't ride well, from Dartmouth

_____ 14. Host

_____ 15. Place where they took the singing boy

_____ 16. Thomas's gift to the friar

_____ 17. What happened to all three youths who found Death

_____ 18. The friar wanted the people to give ____ to pay for trentals

_____ 19. From whom Absalom borrowed an iron

_____ 20. January's wife

The Canterbury Tales Fill In The Blank 3 Answer Key

ARM	1. Carpenter broke his when he fell
CHANTICLEER	2. The cock
BOY	3. He sang
IRE	4. Anger
JOHNNY	5. The fifth husband of the Wife of Bath
WHEEL	6. Squire's suggestion as to how to divide the gift
PARSON	7. Christ-like, patient, giving, holy, virtuous
ALISON	8. Carpenter's wife
KISS	9. Alison agreed to do this to Absalom to make him go away
KNIGHT	10. Had been in many battles, was a gentleman
FIVE	11. Number of husbands the Wife of Bath had
MONK	12. Bald & fat, didn't like work
SHIPMAN	13. Good navigator, didn't ride well, from Dartmouth
BAILLY	14. Host
ABBEY	15. Place where they took the singing boy
GAS	16. Thomas's gift to the friar
DIED	17. What happened to all three youths who found Death
MONEY	18. The friar wanted the people to give ____ to pay for trentals
SMITH	19. From whom Absalom borrowed an iron
MAY	20. January's wife

The Canterbury Tales Fill In The Blank 4

1. What happened to all three youths who found Death
2. The prologue to the Prioress's Tale is a ____
3. He won the contest for Emily's hand
4. The farmer didn't mean his, but the widow did
5. Carpenter broke his when he fell
6. The miller
7. Parish clerk who lusts after Alison
8. Walter brought the ____ back to Griselda
9. The boy's was cut
10. Where the merchant's wife was going to pay him back
11. Simpkin's daughter
12. Griselda was beautiful in looks and ____
13. Good navigator, didn't ride well, from Dartmouth
14. Old, thin, brought up the rear, good manager
15. It came to kill Chanticleer
16. Money paid to the summoner to keep him from making an arrest
17. Football-player build, cheated customers, plays bagpipes
18. What women most desire is ____ over husbands
19. He tricked the miller's wife into sleeping with him
20. Sells false relics, bulging eyes, long yellow hair

The Canterbury Tales Fill In The Blank 4 Answer Key

DIED	1. What happened to all three youths who found Death
PRAYER	2. The prologue to the Prioress's Tale is a ____
ARCITA	3. He won the contest for Emily's hand
CURSE	4. The farmer didn't mean his, but the widow did
ARM	5. Carpenter broke his when he fell
SIMPKIN	6. The miller
ABSALOM	7. Parish clerk who lusts after Alison
CHILDREN	8. Walter brought the ____ back to Griselda
THROAT	9. The boy's was cut
BED	10. Where the merchant's wife was going to pay him back
MOLLY	11. Simpkin's daughter
DEEDS	12. Griselda was beautiful in looks and ____
SHIPMAN	13. Good navigator, didn't ride well, from Dartmouth
REEVE	14. Old, thin, brought up the rear, good manager
FOX	15. It came to kill Chanticleer
BRIBE	16. Money paid to the summoner to keep him from making an arrest
MILLER	17. Football-player build, cheated customers, plays bagpipes
MASTERY	18. What women most desire is ____ over husbands
JOHN	19. He tricked the miller's wife into sleeping with him
PARDONER	20. Sells false relics, bulging eyes, long yellow hair

The Canterbury Tales Matching 1

___ 1. STAB   A. Bald & fat, didn't like work
___ 2. JOHN   B. They were hung under the roof to serve as boats
___ 3. IRE   C. Fiends take different ones to catch their prey
___ 4. FRANCS   D. Squire's suggestion as to how to divide the gift
___ 5. WHEEL   E. Wife of ____
___ 6. PARSON   F. Arveragus tried to help save Dorigen's
___ 7. HONOR   G. Anger
___ 8. SHAPES   H. Had been in many battles, was a gentleman
___ 9. MILLER   I. Liked to eat, drink and be merry
___10. PROLOGUE   J. Christ-like, patient, giving, holy, virtuous
___11. KISS   K. The loan amount: 100 ____
___12. BATH   L. Alison agreed to do this to Absalom to make him go away
___13. THESEUS   M. The older youths planned to do this to the youngest upon his return
___14. YOUNG   N. Place where they took the singing boy
___15. SIMPKIN   O. Emily's brother-in-law; he captured two knights
___16. FAITH   P. Good navigator, didn't ride well, from Dartmouth
___17. FRANKLIN   Q. The miller
___18. ABBEY   R. Number of husbands the Wife of Bath had
___19. THROAT   S. The knight's old woman wife became ____ and beautiful
___20. SHIPMAN   T. The boy's was cut
___21. TUBS   U. Author
___22. MONK   V. The friar told Thomas he had to little of it
___23. FIVE   W. Football-player build, cheated customers, plays bagpipes
___24. KNIGHT   X. He tricked the miller's wife into sleeping with him
___25. CHAUCER   Y. The part that comes before the story

The Canterbury Tales Matching 1 Answer Key

M - 1. STAB	A. Bald & fat, didn't like work
X - 2. JOHN	B. They were hung under the roof to serve as boats
G - 3. IRE	C. Fiends take different ones to catch their prey
K - 4. FRANCS	D. Squire's suggestion as to how to divide the gift
D - 5. WHEEL	E. Wife of _____
J - 6. PARSON	F. Arveragus tried to help save Dorigen's
F - 7. HONOR	G. Anger
C - 8. SHAPES	H. Had been in many battles, was a gentleman
W - 9. MILLER	I. Liked to eat, drink and be merry
Y - 10. PROLOGUE	J. Christ-like, patient, giving, holy, virtuous
L - 11. KISS	K. The loan amount: 100 _____
E - 12. BATH	L. Alison agreed to do this to Absalom to make him go away
O - 13. THESEUS	M. The older youths planned to do this to the youngest upon his return
S - 14. YOUNG	N. Place where they took the singing boy
Q - 15. SIMPKIN	O. Emily's brother-in-law; he captured two knights
V - 16. FAITH	P. Good navigator, didn't ride well, from Dartmouth
I - 17. FRANKLIN	Q. The miller
N - 18. ABBEY	R. Number of husbands the Wife of Bath had
T - 19. THROAT	S. The knight's old woman wife became _____ and beautiful
P - 20. SHIPMAN	T. The boy's was cut
B - 21. TUBS	U. Author
A - 22. MONK	V. The friar told Thomas he had to little of it
R - 23. FIVE	W. Football-player build, cheated customers, plays bagpipes
H - 24. KNIGHT	X. He tricked the miller's wife into sleeping with him
U - 25. CHAUCER	Y. The part that comes before the story

The Canterbury Tales Matching 2

___ 1. BAILLY   A. Emily's brother-in-law; he captured two knights
___ 2. SEA   B. What the miller's wife made from the flour he took from A & J
___ 3. CLERK   C. Loved to learn for the sake of learning
___ 4. CAKE   D. January's wife
___ 5. SEED   E. Christ-like, patient, giving, holy, virtuous
___ 6. DEEDS   F. From whom Absalom borrowed an iron
___ 7. KISS   G. Host
___ 8. PEAR   H. Alison agreed to do this to Absalom to make him go away
___ 9. SMITH   I. The friar wanted the people to give ____ to pay for trentals
___10. YEAR   J. May claimed to desperately want one of this fruit
___11. PRAYER   K. Place where they took the singing boy
___12. REEVE   L. Dainty, pleasant, sensitive, medieval beauty
___13. PARSON   M. Squire's servant
___14. HONOR   N. Author
___15. ABBEY   O. The knight had one ____ and one day to find an answer
___16. PRIORESS   P. Arveragus's castle was near the ____
___17. THESEUS   Q. Griselda was beautiful in looks and ____
___18. MOLLY   R. The prologue to the Prioress's Tale is a ____
___19. MONEY   S. The monk took this from the boy's mouth
___20. TWO   T. Simpkin's daughter
___21. CHAUCER   U. The farmer didn't mean his, but the widow did
___22. TOWER   V. Arveragus tried to help save Dorigen's
___23. YEOMAN   W. Number of years Arveragus was gone
___24. MAY   X. Place where Theseus kept Arcita and Palamon
___25. CURSE   Y. Old, thin, brought up the rear, good manager

The Canterbury Tales Matching 2 Answer Key

G - 1. BAILLY
P - 2. SEA
C - 3. CLERK
B - 4. CAKE
S - 5. SEED
Q - 6. DEEDS
H - 7. KISS
J - 8. PEAR
F - 9. SMITH
O - 10. YEAR
R - 11. PRAYER
Y - 12. REEVE
E - 13. PARSON
V - 14. HONOR
K - 15. ABBEY
L - 16. PRIORESS
A - 17. THESEUS
T - 18. MOLLY
I - 19. MONEY
W - 20. TWO
N - 21. CHAUCER
X - 22. TOWER
M - 23. YEOMAN
D - 24. MAY
U - 25. CURSE

A. Emily's brother-in-law; he captured two knights
B. What the miller's wife made from the flour he took from A & J
C. Loved to learn for the sake of learning
D. January's wife
E. Christ-like, patient, giving, holy, virtuous
F. From whom Absalom borrowed an iron
G. Host
H. Alison agreed to do this to Absalom to make him go away
I. The friar wanted the people to give ____ to pay for trentals
J. May claimed to desperately want one of this fruit
K. Place where they took the singing boy
L. Dainty, pleasant, sensitive, medieval beauty
M. Squire's servant
N. Author
O. The knight had one ____ and one day to find an answer
P. Arveragus's castle was near the ____
Q. Griselda was beautiful in looks and ____
R. The prologue to the Prioress's Tale is a ____
S. The monk took this from the boy's mouth
T. Simpkin's daughter
U. The farmer didn't mean his, but the widow did
V. Arveragus tried to help save Dorigen's
W. Number of years Arveragus was gone
X. Place where Theseus kept Arcita and Palamon
Y. Old, thin, brought up the rear, good manager

The Canterbury Tales Matching 3

___ 1. SEA   A. He slept with the miller's daughter
___ 2. CHILDREN   B. What the miller's wife made from the flour he took from A & J
___ 3. ALLEY   C. Bald & fat, didn't like work
___ 4. MONEY   D. Arveragus tried to help save Dorigen's
___ 5. FRIAR   E. The knight was sent to find the thing women most ____
___ 6. COOK   F. He tried to rid the coast of rocks for Dorigen
___ 7. NICHOLAS   G. Walter brought the ____ back to Griselda
___ 8. THROAT   H. January's wife
___ 9. ABBEY   I. The farmer didn't mean his, but the widow did
___ 10. HONOR   J. The friar wanted the people to give ____ to pay for trentals
___ 11. DESIRE   K. The boy's was cut
___ 12. CAKE   L. Had sores, master chef
___ 13. MAY   M. Place where Theseus kept Arcita and Palamon
___ 14. BOY   N. Place where the singing boy was attacked
___ 15. FRANCS   O. He sang
___ 16. SHAPES   P. He married Emily after his cousin died
___ 17. MONK   Q. Simpkin's daughter
___ 18. ALAN   R. The knight had one ____ and one day to find an answer
___ 19. MOLLY   S. Student boarder with Alison and the carpenter
___ 20. TOWER   T. Arveragus's castle was near the ____
___ 21. PALAMON   U. Loved to learn for the sake of learning
___ 22. CURSE   V. The loan amount: 100 ____
___ 23. AURELIUS   W. Fiends take different ones to catch their prey
___ 24. CLERK   X. Aristocratic, takes bribes for easy penance
___ 25. YEAR   Y. Place where they took the singing boy

The Canterbury Tales Matching 3 Answer Key

T - 1.	SEA	A.	He slept with the miller's daughter
G - 2.	CHILDREN	B.	What the miller's wife made from the flour he took from A & J
N - 3.	ALLEY	C.	Bald & fat, didn't like work
J - 4.	MONEY	D.	Arveragus tried to help save Dorigen's
X - 5.	FRIAR	E.	The knight was sent to find the thing women most ____
L - 6.	COOK	F.	He tried to rid the coast of rocks for Dorigen
S - 7.	NICHOLAS	G.	Walter brought the ____ back to Griselda
K - 8.	THROAT	H.	January's wife
Y - 9.	ABBEY	I.	The farmer didn't mean his, but the widow did
D - 10.	HONOR	J.	The friar wanted the people to give ____ to pay for trentals
E - 11.	DESIRE	K.	The boy's was cut
B - 12.	CAKE	L.	Had sores, master chef
H - 13.	MAY	M.	Place where Theseus kept Arcita and Palamon
O - 14.	BOY	N.	Place where the singing boy was attacked
V - 15.	FRANCS	O.	He sang
W - 16.	SHAPES	P.	He married Emily after his cousin died
C - 17.	MONK	Q.	Simpkin's daughter
A - 18.	ALAN	R.	The knight had one ____ and one day to find an answer
Q - 19.	MOLLY	S.	Student boarder with Alison and the carpenter
M - 20.	TOWER	T.	Arveragus's castle was near the ____
P - 21.	PALAMON	U.	Loved to learn for the sake of learning
I - 22.	CURSE	V.	The loan amount: 100 ____
F - 23.	AURELIUS	W.	Fiends take different ones to catch their prey
U - 24.	CLERK	X.	Aristocratic, takes bribes for easy penance
R - 25.	YEAR	Y.	Place where they took the singing boy

Copyrighted

The Canterbury Tales Matching 4

___ 1. PEAR   A. Forked beard, good negotiator, always told his opinion
___ 2. BRIBE   B. The merchant's wife asked for one from Sir John
___ 3. MAY   C. May claimed to desperately want one of this fruit
___ 4. SUMMONER   D. The cock
___ 5. DESIRE   E. Number of years Arveragus was gone
___ 6. MERCHANT   F. Had sores, master chef
___ 7. FOX   G. It came to kill Chanticleer
___ 8. TOWER   H. Emily's brother-in-law; he captured two knights
___ 9. ARVERAGUS   I. May meets him in a tree
___10. GAS   J. The knight was sent to find the thing women most ____
___11. FRIAR   K. Place where Theseus kept Arcita and Palamon
___12. DAMIAN   L. Money paid to the summoner to keep him from making an arrest
___13. REEVE   M. What the merchant's wife wanted to buy with her loan
___14. NUN   N. What happened to all three youths who found Death
___15. DIED   O. Pertelote, for example
___16. HEN   P. Thomas's gift to the friar
___17. CLOTHES   Q. Old, thin, brought up the rear, good manager
___18. COOK   R. The knight's old woman wife became ____ and beautiful
___19. RELICS   S. ____'s Priest's Tale
___20. TWO   T. Pardoner sells them as remedies
___21. THESEUS   U. Arveragus's castle was near the ____
___22. YOUNG   V. January's wife
___23. SEA   W. Dorigen's husband
___24. LOAN   X. Aristocratic, takes bribes for easy penance
___25. CHANTICLEER   Y. Garland of flowers on head; insulted Friar

The Canterbury Tales Matching 4 Answer Key

C - 1. PEAR	A.	Forked beard, good negotiator, always told his opinion
L - 2. BRIBE	B.	The merchant's wife asked for one from Sir John
V - 3. MAY	C.	May claimed to desperately want one of this fruit
Y - 4. SUMMONER	D.	The cock
J - 5. DESIRE	E.	Number of years Arveragus was gone
A - 6. MERCHANT	F.	Had sores, master chef
G - 7. FOX	G.	It came to kill Chanticleer
K - 8. TOWER	H.	Emily's brother-in-law; he captured two knights
W - 9. ARVERAGUS	I.	May meets him in a tree
P - 10. GAS	J.	The knight was sent to find the thing women most ____
X - 11. FRIAR	K.	Place where Theseus kept Arcita and Palamon
I - 12. DAMIAN	L.	Money paid to the summoner to keep him from making an arrest
Q - 13. REEVE	M.	What the merchant's wife wanted to buy with her loan
S - 14. NUN	N.	What happened to all three youths who found Death
N - 15. DIED	O.	Pertelote, for example
O - 16. HEN	P.	Thomas's gift to the friar
M - 17. CLOTHES	Q.	Old, thin, brought up the rear, good manager
F - 18. COOK	R.	The knight's old woman wife became ____ and beautiful
T - 19. RELICS	S.	____'s Priest's Tale
E - 20. TWO	T.	Pardoner sells them as remedies
H - 21. THESEUS	U.	Arveragus's castle was near the ____
R - 22. YOUNG	V.	January's wife
U - 23. SEA	W.	Dorigen's husband
B - 24. LOAN	X.	Aristocratic, takes bribes for easy penance
D - 25. CHANTICLEER	Y.	Garland of flowers on head; insulted Friar

The Canterbury Tales Magic Squares 1

Match the definition with the vocabulary word. Put your answers in the magic squares below. When your answers are correct, all columns and rows will add to the same number.

A. DEEDS
B. SUMMONER
C. MAY
D. ALAN
E. YEOMAN
F. KNIGHT
G. MONK
H. GAS
I. PRAYER
J. ARVERAGUS
K. BATH
L. DIED
M. TAIL
N. FRANCS
O. FOX
P. BAILLY

1. The loan amount: 100 ____
2. Bald & fat, didn't like work
3. What happened to all three youths who found Death
4. Griselda was beautiful in looks and ____
5. Wife of ____
6. Garland of flowers on head; insulted Friar
7. Place where the friars were hidden in hell
8. Thomas's gift to the friar
9. Squire's servant
10. Host
11. January's wife
12. Dorigen's husband
13. He slept with the miller's daughter
14. The prologue to the Prioress's Tale is a ____
15. Had been in many battles, was a gentleman
16. It came to kill Chanticleer

A=	B=	C=	D=
E=	F=	G=	H=
I=	J=	K=	L=
M=	N=	O=	P=

22
Copyrighted

The Canterbury Tales Magic Squares 1 Answer Key

Match the definition with the vocabulary word. Put your answers in the magic squares below. When your answers are correct, all columns and rows will add to the same number.

A. DEEDS
B. SUMMONER
C. MAY
D. ALAN
E. YEOMAN
F. KNIGHT
G. MONK
H. GAS
I. PRAYER
J. ARVERAGUS
K. BATH
L. DIED
M. TAIL
N. FRANCS
O. FOX
P. BAILLY

1. The loan amount: 100 ____
2. Bald & fat, didn't like work
3. What happened to all three youths who found Death
4. Griselda was beautiful in looks and ____
5. Wife of ____
6. Garland of flowers on head; insulted Friar
7. Place where the friars were hidden in hell
8. Thomas's gift to the friar
9. Squire's servant
10. Host
11. January's wife
12. Dorigen's husband
13. He slept with the miller's daughter
14. The prologue to the Prioress's Tale is a ____
15. Had been in many battles, was a gentleman
16. It came to kill Chanticleer

A=4	B=6	C=11	D=13
E=9	F=15	G=2	H=8
I=14	J=12	K=5	L=3
M=7	N=1	O=16	P=10

The Canterbury Tales Magic Squares 2

Match the definition with the vocabulary word. Put your answers in the magic squares below. When your answers are correct, all columns and rows will add to the same number.

A. LOAN
B. CLERK
C. SQUIRE
D. PARSON
E. BOW
F. BAILLY
G. FRIAR
H. HONOR
I. TAIL
J. STAB
K. GAS
L. FIVE
M. WHEEL
N. TUBS
O. SMITH
P. THESEUS

1. Squire's suggestion as to how to divide the gift
2. Host
3. Arveragus tried to help save Dorigen's
4. From whom Absalom borrowed an iron
5. Number of husbands the Wife of Bath had
6. Son of the knight
7. The merchant's wife asked for one from Sir John
8. The older youths planned to do this to the youngest upon his return
9. Thomas's gift to the friar
10. Christ-like, patient, giving, holy, virtuous
11. Loved to learn for the sake of learning
12. Place where the friars were hidden in hell
13. They were hung under the roof to serve as boats
14. Arcita fell onto his and broke his breast
15. Aristocratic, takes bribes for easy penance
16. Emily's brother-in-law; he captured two knights

A=	B=	C=	D=
E=	F=	G=	H=
I=	J=	K=	L=
M=	N=	O=	P=

The Canterbury Tales Magic Squares 2 Answer Key

Match the definition with the vocabulary word. Put your answers in the magic squares below. When your answers are correct, all columns and rows will add to the same number.

A. LOAN
B. CLERK
C. SQUIRE
D. PARSON
E. BOW
F. BAILLY
G. FRIAR
H. HONOR
I. TAIL
J. STAB
K. GAS
L. FIVE
M. WHEEL
N. TUBS
O. SMITH
P. THESEUS

1. Squire's suggestion as to how to divide the gift
2. Host
3. Arveragus tried to help save Dorigen's
4. From whom Absalom borrowed an iron
5. Number of husbands the Wife of Bath had
6. Son of the knight
7. The merchant's wife asked for one from Sir John
8. The older youths planned to do this to the youngest upon his return
9. Thomas's gift to the friar
10. Christ-like, patient, giving, holy, virtuous
11. Loved to learn for the sake of learning
12. Place where the friars were hidden in hell
13. They were hung under the roof to serve as boats
14. Arcita fell onto his and broke his breast
15. Aristocratic, takes bribes for easy penance
16. Emily's brother-in-law; he captured two knights

A=7	B=11	C=6	D=10
E=14	F=2	G=15	H=3
I=12	J=8	K=9	L=5
M=1	N=13	O=4	P=16

The Canterbury Tales Magic Squares 3

Match the definition with the vocabulary word. Put your answers in the magic squares below. When your answers are correct, all columns and rows will add to the same number.

A. HEN
B. GRISELDA
C. PROLOGUE
D. HONOR
E. ABSALOM
F. SEA
G. FAITH
H. PRAYER
I. MONK
J. MASTERY
K. DEEDS
L. SUMMONER
M. FIEND
N. DIED
O. ALLEY
P. SMITH

1. The part that comes before the story
2. What women most desire is ____ over husbands
3. Arveragus's castle was near the ____
4. Place where the singing boy was attacked
5. From whom Absalom borrowed an iron
6. Parish clerk who lusts after Alison
7. Bald & fat, didn't like work
8. Arveragus tried to help save Dorigen's
9. The yeoman's true identity
10. The prologue to the Prioress's Tale is a ____
11. Garland of flowers on head; insulted Friar
12. Pertelote, for example
13. Marquis' new wife
14. Griselda was beautiful in looks and ____
15. The friar told Thomas he had to little of it
16. What happened to all three youths who found Death

A=	B=	C=	D=
E=	F=	G=	H=
I=	J=	K=	L=
M=	N=	O=	P=

The Canterbury Tales Magic Squares 3 Answer Key

Match the definition with the vocabulary word. Put your answers in the magic squares below. When your answers are correct, all columns and rows will add to the same number.

A. HEN
B. GRISELDA
C. PROLOGUE
D. HONOR
E. ABSALOM
F. SEA
G. FAITH
H. PRAYER
I. MONK
J. MASTERY
K. DEEDS
L. SUMMONER
M. FIEND
N. DIED
O. ALLEY
P. SMITH

1. The part that comes before the story
2. What women most desire is ____ over husbands
3. Arveragus's castle was near the ____
4. Place where the singing boy was attacked
5. From whom Absalom borrowed an iron
6. Parish clerk who lusts after Alison
7. Bald & fat, didn't like work
8. Arveragus tried to help save Dorigen's
9. The yeoman's true identity
10. The prologue to the Prioress's Tale is a ____
11. Garland of flowers on head; insulted Friar
12. Pertelote, for example
13. Marquis' new wife
14. Griselda was beautiful in looks and ____
15. The friar told Thomas he had to little of it
16. What happened to all three youths who found Death

A=12	B=13	C=1	D=8
E=6	F=3	G=15	H=10
I=7	J=2	K=14	L=11
M=9	N=16	O=4	P=5

The Canterbury Tales Magic Squares 4

Match the definition with the vocabulary word. Put your answers in the magic squares below. When your answers are correct, all columns and rows will add to the same number.

A. DRUNK
B. CAKE
C. MERCHANT
D. YEOMAN
E. REEVE
F. MAY
G. JOHNNY
H. SQUIRE
I. BATH
J. PRAYER
K. CLOTHES
L. NICHOLAS
M. BRIBE
N. SHIPMAN
O. YOUNG
P. YEAR

1. Son of the knight
2. Condition of the Miller as he told his tale
3. What the miller's wife made from the flour he took from A & J
4. The fifth husband of the Wife of Bath
5. The prologue to the Prioress's Tale is a ____
6. The knight's old woman wife became ____ and beautiful
7. The knight had one ____ and one day to find an answer
8. Wife of ____
9. What the merchant's wife wanted to buy with her loan
10. Good navigator, didn't ride well, from Dartmouth
11. Money paid to the summoner to keep him from making an arrest
12. Student boarder with Alison and the carpenter
13. Old, thin, brought up the rear, good manager
14. Squire's servant
15. Forked beard, good negotiator, always told his opinion
16. January's wife

A=	B=	C=	D=
E=	F=	G=	H=
I=	J=	K=	L=
M=	N=	O=	P=

The Canterbury Tales Magic Squares 4 Answer Key

Match the definition with the vocabulary word. Put your answers in the magic squares below. When your answers are correct, all columns and rows will add to the same number.

A. DRUNK
B. CAKE
C. MERCHANT
D. YEOMAN
E. REEVE
F. MAY
G. JOHNNY
H. SQUIRE
I. BATH
J. PRAYER
K. CLOTHES
L. NICHOLAS
M. BRIBE
N. SHIPMAN
O. YOUNG
P. YEAR

1. Son of the knight
2. Condition of the Miller as he told his tale
3. What the miller's wife made from the flour he took from A & J
4. The fifth husband of the Wife of Bath
5. The prologue to the Prioress's Tale is a ____
6. The knight's old woman wife became ____ and beautiful
7. The knight had one ____ and one day to find an answer
8. Wife of ____
9. What the merchant's wife wanted to buy with her loan
10. Good navigator, didn't ride well, from Dartmouth
11. Money paid to the summoner to keep him from making an arrest
12. Student boarder with Alison and the carpenter
13. Old, thin, brought up the rear, good manager
14. Squire's servant
15. Forked beard, good negotiator, always told his opinion
16. January's wife

A=2	B=3	C=15	D=14
E=13	F=16	G=4	H=1
I=8	J=5	K=9	L=12
M=11	N=10	O=6	P=7

The Canterbury Tales Word Search 1

```
K S P S H I P M A N E Y E S T L B
C N S E T E A E I R C B V C T I J
N I I G A Y N R I L I F I I B A P
K T Z G B R Y C T R L P F L E T B
C A K E H S O H B P T E D E D G T
L Q A D C T U A O R O U R R R O M
P B L N F D N N W O W C B D U L L
P R A Y E R G T V L E X E S N D M
M R N I K I I T F O R I H P K V S
F J M W L Q R A F G D A A N F Q B
A R D O N L I O R U P R N H O J Z
L B E W L T Y S N E D H Y Y X O G
I Z S T H L V S S O R A E Y N H V
S H I A O Z Y K N K S M N V A N P
O E R V L B N E J A C R O R O N N
N S E A D O R I G E N E M I L Y D
N U N D M Y M P R I O R E S S K H
```

Alison agreed to do this to Absalom to make him go away (4)
Anger (3)
Arcita fell onto his and broke his breast (3)
Aristocratic, takes bribes for easy penance (5)
Arveragus's castle was near the ____ (3)
Bald & fat, didn't like work (4)
Carpenter broke his when he fell (3)
Carpenter's wife (6)
Chanticleer closed his when he began to sing (4)
Condition of the Miller as he told his tale (5)
Dainty, pleasant, sensitive, medieval beauty (8)
Fiends take different ones to catch their prey (6)
Football-player build, cheated customers, plays bagpipes (6)
Forked beard, good negotiator, always told his opinion (8)
Good navigator, didn't ride well, from Dartmouth (7)
Had been in many battles, was a gentleman (6)
He sang (3)
He slept with the miller's daughter (4)
He tricked the miller's wife into sleeping with him (4)
Host (6)
It branded Nicholas (4)
It came to kill Chanticleer (3)
It was under the tree (5)
January's wife (3)
May claimed to desperately want one of this fruit (4)
Money paid to the summoner to keep him from making an arrest (5)
Number of husbands the Wife of Bath had (4)
Number of years Arveragus was gone (3)
Pardoner sells them as remedies (6)
Parish clerk who lusts after Alison (7)
Pertelote, for example (3)

Place where Theseus kept Arcita and Palamon (5)
Place where the friars were hidden in hell (4)
Sells false relics, bulging eyes, long yellow hair (8)
She missed Arveragus (7)
Simpkin's daughter (5)
The Wife of Bath married Johnny for this, not money (4)
The fifth husband of the Wife of Bath (6)
The friar told Thomas he had to little of it (5)
The friar wanted the people to give ____ to pay for trentals (5)
The knight had one ____ and one day to find an answer (4)
The knight was sent to find the thing women most ____ (6)
The knight's old woman wife became ____ and beautiful (5)
The loan amount: 100 ____ (6)
The merchant's wife asked for one from Sir John (4)
The monk took this from the boy's mouth (4)
The older youths planned to do this to the youngest upon his return (4)
The part that comes before the story (8)
The prologue to the Prioress's Tale is a ____ (6)
The queen's sister; two knights loved her (5)
They were hung under the roof to serve as boats (4)
Thomas's gift to the friar (3)
What happened to all three youths who found Death (4)
What the miller's wife made from the flour he took from A & J (4)
Where the merchant's wife was going to pay him back (3)
Wife of ____ (4)
____'s Priest's Tale (3)

The Canterbury Tales Word Search 1 Answer Key

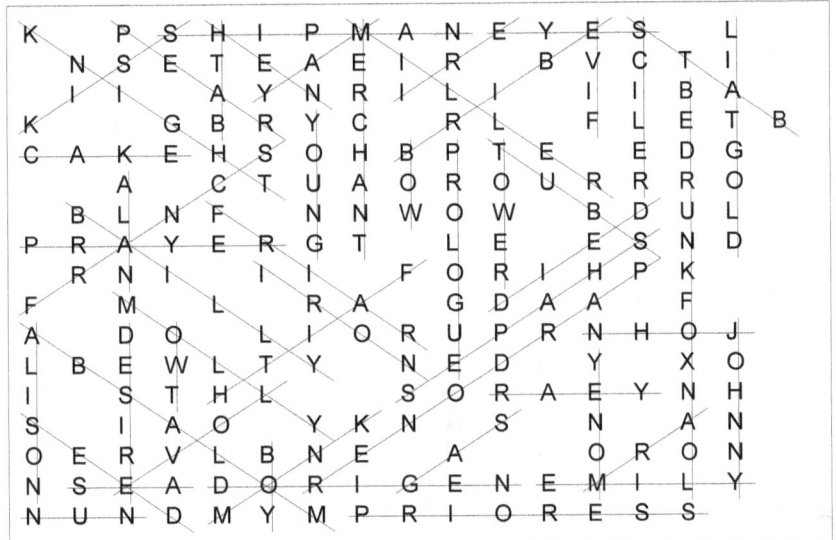

Alison agreed to do this to Absalom to make him go away (4)
Anger (3)
Arcita fell onto his and broke his breast (3)
Aristocratic, takes bribes for easy penance (5)
Arveragus's castle was near the ____ (3)
Bald & fat, didn't like work (4)
Carpenter broke his when he fell (3)
Carpenter's wife (6)
Chanticleer closed his when he began to sing (4)
Condition of the Miller as he told his tale (5)
Dainty, pleasant, sensitive, medieval beauty (8)
Fiends take different ones to catch their prey (6)
Football-player build, cheated customers, plays bagpipes (6)
Forked beard, good negotiator, always told his opinion (8)
Good navigator, didn't ride well, from Dartmouth (7)
Had been in many battles, was a gentleman (6)
He sang (3)
He slept with the miller's daughter (4)
He tricked the miller's wife into sleeping with him (4)
Host (6)
It branded Nicholas (4)
It came to kill Chanticleer (3)
It was under the tree (5)
January's wife (3)
May claimed to desperately want one of this fruit (4)
Money paid to the summoner to keep him from making an arrest (5)
Number of husbands the Wife of Bath had (4)
Number of years Arveragus was gone (3)
Pardoner sells them as remedies (6)
Parish clerk who lusts after Alison (7)
Pertelote, for example (3)

Place where Theseus kept Arcita and Palamon (5)
Place where the friars were hidden in hell (4)
Sells false relics, bulging eyes, long yellow hair (8)
She missed Arveragus (7)
Simpkin's daughter (5)
The Wife of Bath married Johnny for this, not money (4)
The fifth husband of the Wife of Bath (6)
The friar told Thomas he had to little of it (5)
The friar wanted the people to give ____ to pay for trentals (5)
The knight had one ____ and one day to find an answer (4)
The knight was sent to find the thing women most ____ (6)
The knight's old woman wife became ____ and beautiful (5)
The loan amount: 100 ____ (6)
The merchant's wife asked for one from Sir John (4)
The monk took this from the boy's mouth (4)
The older youths planned to do this to the youngest upon his return (4)
The part that comes before the story (8)
The prologue to the Prioress's Tale is a ____ (6)
The queen's sister; two knights loved her (5)
They were hung under the roof to serve as boats (4)
Thomas's gift to the friar (3)
What happened to all three youths who found Death (4)
What the miller's wife made from the flour he took from A & J (4)
Where the merchant's wife was going to pay him back (3)
Wife of ____ (4)
____'s Priest's Tale (3)

The Canterbury Tales Word Search 2

```
F R A N K L I N C L O T H E S S W
I B B A P H E I C W H D R R A E H
E Y O L C G P K T C L I B I L E E
N Y Y A I A G P D O U F Y S O D E
D F K R K U F M G Q E R U E H A L
L E O R N R T I S B O M S D C R P
P D E X I E T S I N M Y Q E I M A
N L H A G L U R O O Y B Y J N T R
C T R B H I B H N Y E L L A O W D
P O A Q T U S E Y B O W L D D H O
R W E B R S R P E G S H I P M A N
O E P Y A L Q L O I G E A N F U E
L R E C B T O P M R D R B I N R R
O B P V B V H A A O B A V Q L K C
G R I S E L D A N N R E L L I M O
U A S E Y E E X E G R Y D S A A O
E C S U E S E H T I M S S C T Y K
```

Alison agreed to do this to Absalom to make him go away (4)
Anger (3)
Arcita fell onto his and broke his breast (3)
Aristocratic, takes bribes for easy penance (5)
Arveragus tried to help save Dorigen's (5)
Arveragus's castle was near the ____ (3)
Carpenter broke his when he fell (3)
Chanticleer closed his when he began to sing (4)
Emily's brother-in-law; he captured two knights (7)
Football-player build, cheated customers, plays bagpipes (6)
From whom Absalom borrowed an iron (5)
Garland of flowers on head; insulted Friar (8)
Good navigator, didn't ride well, from Dartmouth (7)
Had been in many battles, was a gentleman (6)
Had sores, master chef (4)
He sang (3)
He slept with the miller's daughter (4)
He tricked the miller's wife into sleeping with him (4)
He tried to rid the coast of rocks for Dorigen (8)
Host (6)
It branded Nicholas (4)
It came to kill Chanticleer (3)
It was under the tree (5)
January's wife (3)
Liked to eat, drink and be merry (8)
Loved to learn for the sake of learning (5)
Marquis' new wife (8)
May claimed to desperately want one of this fruit (4)
Money paid to the summoner to keep him from making an arrest (5)
Number of husbands the Wife of Bath had (4)
Number of years Arveragus was gone (3)
Old, thin, brought up the rear, good manager (5)

Pertelote, for example (3)
Place where Theseus kept Arcita and Palamon (5)
Place where the friars were hidden in hell (4)
Place where the singing boy was attacked (5)
Place where they took the singing boy (5)
Sells false relics, bulging eyes, long yellow hair (8)
She missed Arveragus (7)
Son of the knight (6)
Squire's servant (6)
Squire's suggestion as to how to divide the gift (5)
Student boarder with Alison and the carpenter (8)
The Wife of Bath married Johnny for this, not money (4)
The farmer didn't mean his, but the widow did (5)
The knight had one ____ and one day to find an answer (4)
The knight was sent to find the thing women most ____ (6)
The merchant's wife asked for one from Sir John (4)
The miller (7)
The monk took this from the boy's mouth (4)
The part that comes before the story (8)
The yeoman's true identity (5)
They were hung under the roof to serve as boats (4)
Thomas's gift to the friar (3)
What happened to all three youths who found Death (4)
What the merchant's wife wanted to buy with her loan (7)
What the miller's wife made from the flour he took from A & J (4)
Where the merchant's wife was going to pay him back (3)
Wife of ____ (4)
____'s Priest's Tale (3)

The Canterbury Tales Word Search 2 Answer Key

Alison agreed to do this to Absalom to make him go away (4)
Anger (3)
Arcita fell onto his and broke his breast (3)
Aristocratic, takes bribes for easy penance (5)
Arveragus tried to help save Dorigen's (5)
Arveragus's castle was near the ____ (3)
Carpenter broke his when he fell (3)
Chanticleer closed his when he began to sing (4)
Emily's brother-in-law; he captured two knights (7)
Football-player build, cheated customers, plays bagpipes (6)
From whom Absalom borrowed an iron (5)
Garland of flowers on head; insulted Friar (8)
Good navigator, didn't ride well, from Dartmouth (7)
Had been in many battles, was a gentleman (6)
Had sores, master chef (4)
He sang (3)
He slept with the miller's daughter (4)
He tricked the miller's wife into sleeping with him (4)
He tried to rid the coast of rocks for Dorigen (8)
Host (6)
It branded Nicholas (4)
It came to kill Chanticleer (3)
It was under the tree (5)
January's wife (3)
Liked to eat, drink and be merry (8)
Loved to learn for the sake of learning (5)
Marquis' new wife (8)
May claimed to desperately want one of this fruit (4)
Money paid to the summoner to keep him from making an arrest (5)
Number of husbands the Wife of Bath had (4)
Number of years Arveragus was gone (3)
Old, thin, brought up the rear, good manager (5)

Pertelote, for example (3)
Place where Theseus kept Arcita and Palamon (5)
Place where the friars were hidden in hell (4)
Place where the singing boy was attacked (5)
Place where they took the singing boy (5)
Sells false relics, bulging eyes, long yellow hair (8)
She missed Arveragus (7)
Son of the knight (6)
Squire's servant (6)
Squire's suggestion as to how to divide the gift (5)
Student boarder with Alison and the carpenter (8)
The Wife of Bath married Johnny for this, not money (4)
The farmer didn't mean his, but the widow did (5)
The knight had one ____ and one day to find an answer (4)
The knight was sent to find the thing women most ____ (6)
The merchant's wife asked for one from Sir John (4)
The miller (7)
The monk took this from the boy's mouth (4)
The part that comes before the story (8)
The yeoman's true identity (5)
They were hung under the roof to serve as boats (4)
Thomas's gift to the friar (3)
What happened to all three youths who found Death (4)
What the merchant's wife wanted to buy with her loan (7)
What the miller's wife made from the flour he took from A & J (4)
Where the merchant's wife was going to pay him back (3)
Wife of ____ (4)
____'s Priest's Tale (3)

The Canterbury Tales Word Search 3

```
A R V E R A G U S C I L E R F A I T H B
B A G T F M V N S M J E F K Z C T R Y Q
B L R A Z R I P I R Y M C O J R A Y N D
E I I T D C I L K I S I O C X E O D N M
Y E S I T U W A L R F L O E L W R E H M
P Y E C H I L D R E N Y K S G O H B O Y
H C L R E R R T Y H R A E A G T T E J Y
T G D A S O E E E T C P R G A J D H N J
I V A C E N S E N R A D E B Y K E O E D
M O N K U J N N V H Y D N E I F S Y B S
S O D F S R A Q S E C E O C R R I E I C
G H N H H I S N P X G M M N A Z R A R H
N G L E M J G E A I A L M P U S E R B C
N A L A Y O W N R N D R U N K N T W O L
S J D Y L H P O D A P S S F I A R A G R
V E N D E N D C O O E E C K I E B B B Z
W R E E T U B S N L A A P L Y S D E E D
H K L D C F B P E L R M M A E E C V A F
F R A N C S C O R X I H R A I R I O R G
M E R C H A N T W S V P D D Y F K L M L
```

ABBEY	DAMIAN	IRE	RELICS
ADULTERY	DEEDS	IRON	SEA
ALAN	DESIRE	JOHN	SEED
ALLEY	DIED	JOHNNY	SHAPES
ARCITA	DORIGEN	KISS	SIMPKIN
ARM	DRUNK	LOAN	SMITH
ARVERAGUS	EMILY	LOVE	STAB
BATH	EYES	MAY	SUMMONER
BED	FAITH	MERCHANT	TAIL
BOW	FIEND	MILLER	THESEUS
BOY	FIVE	MONEY	THROAT
BRIBE	FOX	MONK	TOWER
CAKE	FRANCS	NUN	TUBS
CHILDREN	FRIAR	PARDONER	TWO
CLERK	GAS	PARSON	WHEEL
CLOTHES	GOLD	PEAR	YEAR
COOK	GRISELDA	PRAYER	YEOMAN
CURSE	HEN	REEVE	

The Canterbury Tales Word Search 3 Answer Key

ABBEY	DAMIAN	IRE	RELICS
ADULTERY	DEEDS	IRON	SEA
ALAN	DESIRE	JOHN	SEED
ALLEY	DIED	JOHNNY	SHAPES
ARCITA	DORIGEN	KISS	SIMPKIN
ARM	DRUNK	LOAN	SMITH
ARVERAGUS	EMILY	LOVE	STAB
BATH	EYES	MAY	SUMMONER
BED	FAITH	MERCHANT	TAIL
BOW	FIEND	MILLER	THESEUS
BOY	FIVE	MONEY	THROAT
BRIBE	FOX	MONK	TOWER
CAKE	FRANCS	NUN	TUBS
CHILDREN	FRIAR	PARDONER	TWO
CLERK	GAS	PARSON	WHEEL
CLOTHES	GOLD	PEAR	YEAR
COOK	GRISELDA	PRAYER	YEOMAN
CURSE	HEN	REEVE	

The Canterbury Tales Word Search 4

```
S H I P M A N I L K N A R F R I A R A M
C T C P A R S O N I Y U A Q I T A N L G
N H L Q R L B B C E R I N C I E S E L S
A R E H E W A H O F T W Y C Y K N R E S
R O R P C K O M K H E B R G O L D D Y Q
F A K U U L A N O N R A R O D S I L R N
V T R N A N O S D N I S C I B D E I E S
X S A S H M M T D R U G T Q B E D H T J
E L L E C R V J H E Q T H A P E Y C S D
K O A U A S R T S E S K K T I D O Y A Y
G V N G Q S I E R S S I I J M L U B M S
R E W O T M H E L P B Y R S R K N A O L
T W J L S T Y C K I A A Y E S E G B F L
U M G O Y A L A N D C R I A B B E Y I M
B A X R R P F K E T J S D L K E P V V Y
S H A P E S N E G I R O D O L D I R E X
Z I M S E N S H Y G A J H E N Y R N Q P
F R W F T A T T D E E O E N Y E O U N M
H O N O R A R V W P S H Y A N M R E N Y
B N X N B W B O Y O W N M L L Y H B X K
```

ABBEY	DESIRE	JOHNNY	SEA
ALAN	DIED	KISS	SEED
ALLEY	DORIGEN	KNIGHT	SHAPES
ARCITA	DRUNK	LOAN	SHIPMAN
ARM	EYES	LOVE	SMITH
BAILLY	FAITH	MASTERY	SQUIRE
BATH	FIEND	MAY	STAB
BED	FIVE	MONEY	TAIL
BOW	FOX	MONK	THESEUS
BOY	FRANCS	NICHOLAS	THROAT
BRIBE	FRANKLIN	NUN	TOWER
CAKE	FRIAR	PALAMON	TUBS
CHAUCER	GAS	PARDONER	TWO
CHILDREN	GOLD	PARSON	WHEEL
CLERK	HEN	PEAR	YEAR
CLOTHES	HONOR	PRAYER	YEOMAN
COOK	IRE	PROLOGUE	YOUNG
CURSE	IRON	REEVE	
DEEDS	JOHN	RELICS	

The Canterbury Tales Magic Squares 4 Answer Key

ABBEY	DESIRE	JOHNNY	SEA
ALAN	DIED	KISS	SEED
ALLEY	DORIGEN	KNIGHT	SHAPES
ARCITA	DRUNK	LOAN	SHIPMAN
ARM	EYES	LOVE	SMITH
BAILLY	FAITH	MASTERY	SQUIRE
BATH	FIEND	MAY	STAB
BED	FIVE	MONEY	TAIL
BOW	FOX	MONK	THESEUS
BOY	FRANCS	NICHOLAS	THROAT
BRIBE	FRANKLIN	NUN	TOWER
CAKE	FRIAR	PALAMON	TUBS
CHAUCER	GAS	PARDONER	TWO
CHILDREN	GOLD	PARSON	WHEEL
CLERK	HEN	PEAR	YEAR
CLOTHES	HONOR	PRAYER	YEOMAN
COOK	IRE	PROLOGUE	YOUNG
CURSE	IRON	REEVE	
DEEDS	JOHN	RELICS	

The Canterbury Tales Crossword 1

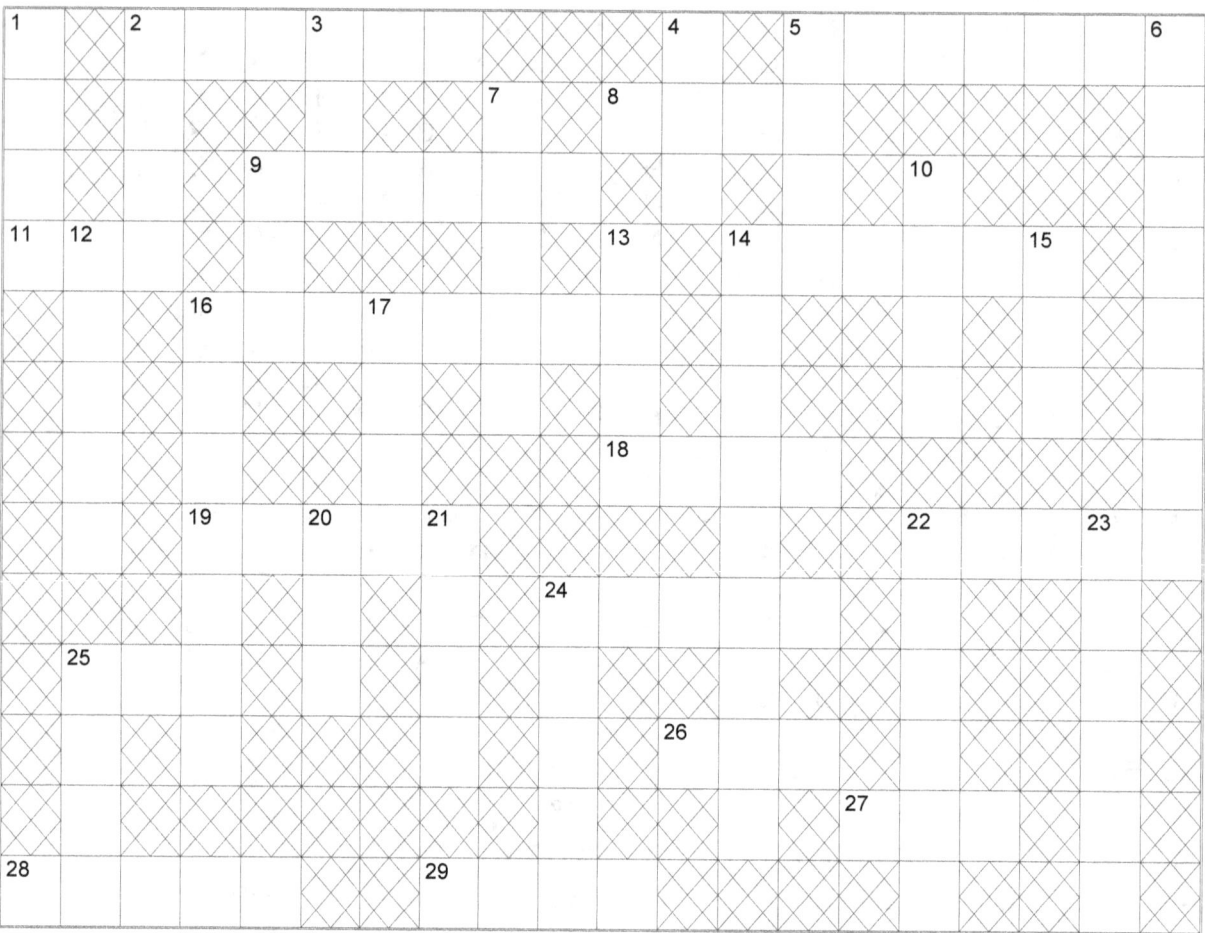

Across
2. Carpenter's wife
5. He married Emily after his cousin died
8. What the miller's wife made from the flour he took from A & J
9. Host
11. Pertelote, for example
14. He won the contest for Emily's hand
16. A young wife would help January from committing this sin
18. The monk took this from the boy's mouth
19. Place where they took the singing boy
22. Griselda was beautiful in looks and ____
24. Aristocratic, takes bribes for easy penance
25. Number of years Arveragus was gone
26. ____'s Priest's Tale
27. January's wife
28. Loved to learn for the sake of learning
29. He tricked the miller's wife into sleeping with him

Down
1. Wife of ____
2. He slept with the miller's daughter
3. Arveragus's castle was near the ____
4. Thomas's gift to the friar
5. May claimed to desperately want one of this fruit
6. Student boarder with Alison and the carpenter
7. Place where the singing boy was attacked
9. Where the merchant's wife was going to pay him back
10. What happened to all three youths who found Death
12. The queen's sister; two knights loved her
13. Chanticleer closed his when he began to sing
14. Dorigen's husband
15. Carpenter broke his when he fell
16. Parish clerk who lusts after Alison
17. The Wife of Bath married Johnny for this, not money
20. Arcita fell onto his and broke his breast
21. The knight had one ____ and one day to find an answer
22. May meets him in a tree
23. The knight was sent to find the thing women most ____
24. The friar told Thomas he had to little of it
25. Place where the friars were hidden in hell

The Canterbury Tales Crossword 1 Answer Key

	1 B		2 A	L	3 I	S	O	N		4 G		5 P	A	L	A	M	O	6 N
	A		L			E		7 A	8 C	A	K	E						I
	T		A		9 B	A	I	L	L	Y		S		A		10 D		C
11 H	12 E	N		E				L		13 E	14 A	R	C	I	T	15 A		H
	M		16 A	D	17 U	L	T	E	R	Y	R			E		R		O
	I		B		O		Y			E	V			D		M		L
	L		S		V			18 S	E	E	D							A
	Y		19 A	20 B	21 B	E	Y			R			22 D	E	E	23 D	S
			L	O	E			24 F	R	I	A	R	A			E	
	25 T	W	O	W	A			A			G		M			S	
	A		M		R		I			26 N	U	N	I			I	
	I				T					S		27 M	A	Y		R	
28 C	L	E	R	K		29 J	O	H	N			N				E	

Across

2. Carpenter's wife
5. He married Emily after his cousin died
8. What the miller's wife made from the flour he took from A & J
9. Host
11. Pertelote, for example
14. He won the contest for Emily's hand
16. A young wife would help January from committing this sin
18. The monk took this from the boy's mouth
19. Place where they took the singing boy
22. Griselda was beautiful in looks and ____
24. Aristocratic, takes bribes for easy penance
25. Number of years Arveragus was gone
26. ____'s Priest's Tale
27. January's wife
28. Loved to learn for the sake of learning
29. He tricked the miller's wife into sleeping with him

Down

1. Wife of ____
2. He slept with the miller's daughter
3. Arveragus's castle was near the ____
4. Thomas's gift to the friar
5. May claimed to desperately want one of this fruit
6. Student boarder with Alison and the carpenter
7. Place where the singing boy was attacked
9. Where the merchant's wife was going to pay him back
10. What happened to all three youths who found Death
12. The queen's sister; two knights loved her
13. Chanticleer closed his when he began to sing
14. Dorigen's husband
15. Carpenter broke his when he fell
16. Parish clerk who lusts after Alison
17. The Wife of Bath married Johnny for this, not money
20. Arcita fell onto his and broke his breast
21. The knight had one ____ and one day to find an answer
22. May meets him in a tree
23. The knight was sent to find the thing women most ____
24. The friar told Thomas he had to little of it
25. Place where the friars were hidden in hell

The Canterbury Tales Word Search 2

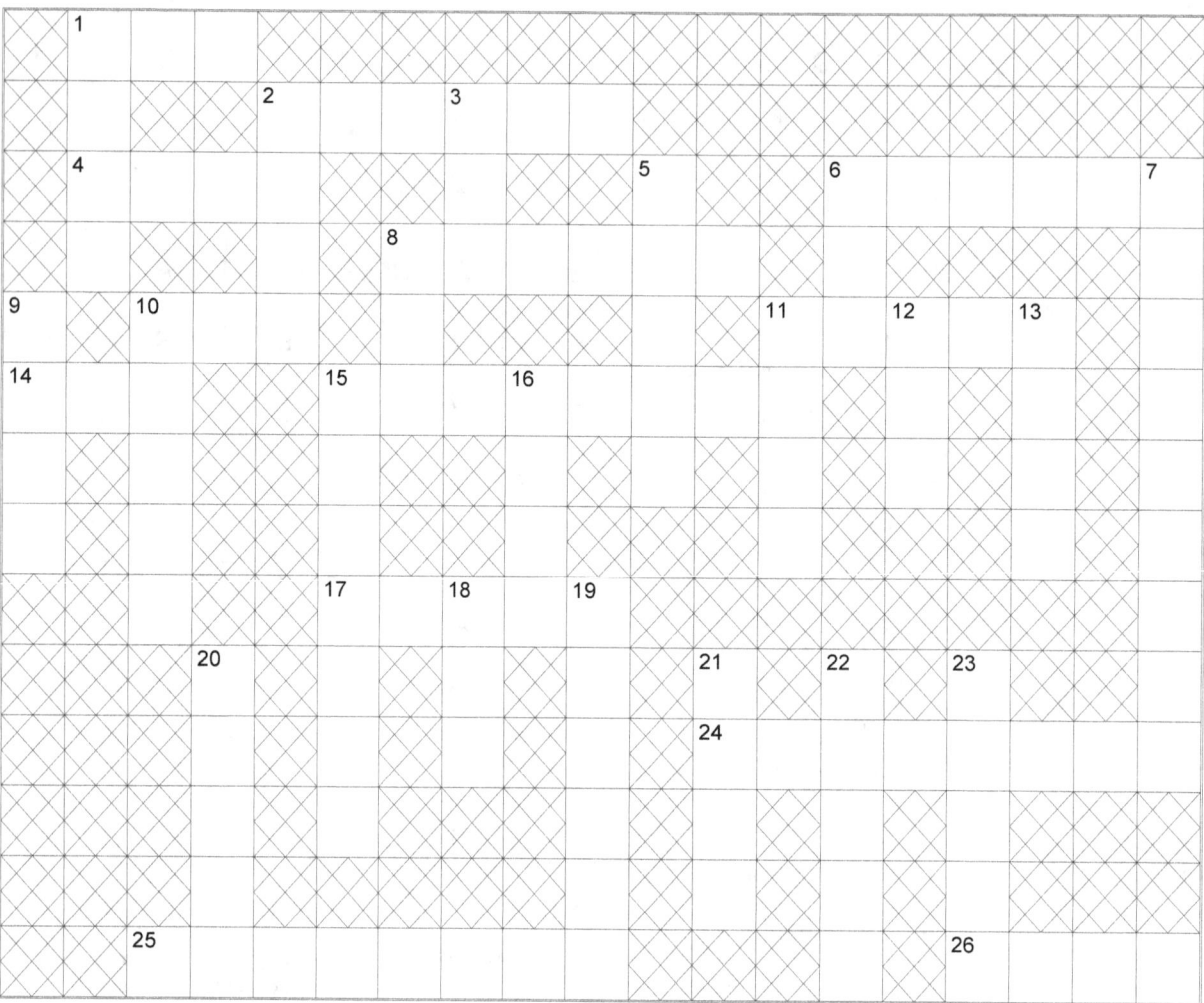

Across
1. Arcita fell onto his and broke his breast
2. Carpenter's wife
4. Place where the friars were hidden in hell
6. He won the contest for Emily's hand
8. Host
10. Pertelote, for example
11. The queen's sister; two knights loved her
14. Number of years Arveragus was gone
15. A young wife would help January from committing this sin
17. Place where they took the singing boy
24. He tried to rid the coast of rocks for Dorigen
25. Walter brought the ____ back to Griselda
26. Alison agreed to do this to Absalom to make him go away

Down
1. Wife of ____
2. He slept with the miller's daughter
3. Arveragus's castle was near the ____
5. Place where the singing boy was attacked
6. Carpenter broke his when he fell
7. Dorigen's husband
8. Where the merchant's wife was going to pay him back
9. The older youths planned to do this to the youngest upon his return
10. Arveragus tried to help save Dorigen's
11. Chanticleer closed his when he began to sing
12. Anger
13. The knight had one ____ and one day to find an answer
15. Parish clerk who lusts after Alison
16. The Wife of Bath married Johnny for this, not money
18. He sang
19. Squire's servant
20. The friar told Thomas he had to little of it
21. What the miller's wife made from the flour he took from A & J
22. Money paid to the summoner to keep him from making an arrest
23. Loved to learn for the sake of learning

The Canterbury Tales Crossword 2 Answer Key

	1 B	O	W										
	A			2 A	L	3 I	S	O	N				
	4 T	A	I	L		E		5 A		6 A	R	C	7 I	T	A
	H			A	8 B	A	I	L	L	Y			R
9 S		10 H	E	N		E		L		11 E	12 M	13 I	L	Y		V
14 T	W	O		15 A	D	U	16 L	T	E	R	Y		R		E		E
A		N		B			O		Y		E		E		A		R
B		O		S			V				S				R		A
		R			17 A	18 B	B	19 E	Y								G
			20 F	L	O	Y	E			21 C	22 B		23 C		U
			A		O	Y	O		24 A	U	R	E	L	I	U	S
			I		M		M			K	I		E		
			T				A			E	B		R		
		25 C	H	I	L	D	R	E	N		E		26 K	I	S	S

Across
1. Arcita fell onto his and broke his breast
2. Carpenter's wife
4. Place where the friars were hidden in hell
6. He won the contest for Emily's hand
8. Host
10. Pertelote, for example
11. The queen's sister; two knights loved her
14. Number of years Arveragus was gone
15. A young wife would help January from committing this sin
17. Place where they took the singing boy
24. He tried to rid the coast of rocks for Dorigen
25. Walter brought the ____ back to Griselda
26. Alison agreed to do this to Absalom to make him go away

Down
1. Wife of ____
2. He slept with the miller's daughter
3. Arveragus's castle was near the ____
5. Place where the singing boy was attacked
6. Carpenter broke his when he fell
7. Dorigen's husband
8. Where the merchant's wife was going to pay him back
9. The older youths planned to do this to the youngest upon his return
10. Arveragus tried to help save Dorigen's
11. Chanticleer closed his when he began to sing
12. Anger
13. The knight had one ____ and one day to find an answer
15. Parish clerk who lusts after Alison
16. The Wife of Bath married Johnny for this, not money
18. He sang
19. Squire's servant
20. The friar told Thomas he had to little of it
21. What the miller's wife made from the flour he took from A & J
22. Money paid to the summoner to keep him from making an arrest
23. Loved to learn for the sake of learning

The Canterbury Tales Crossword 3

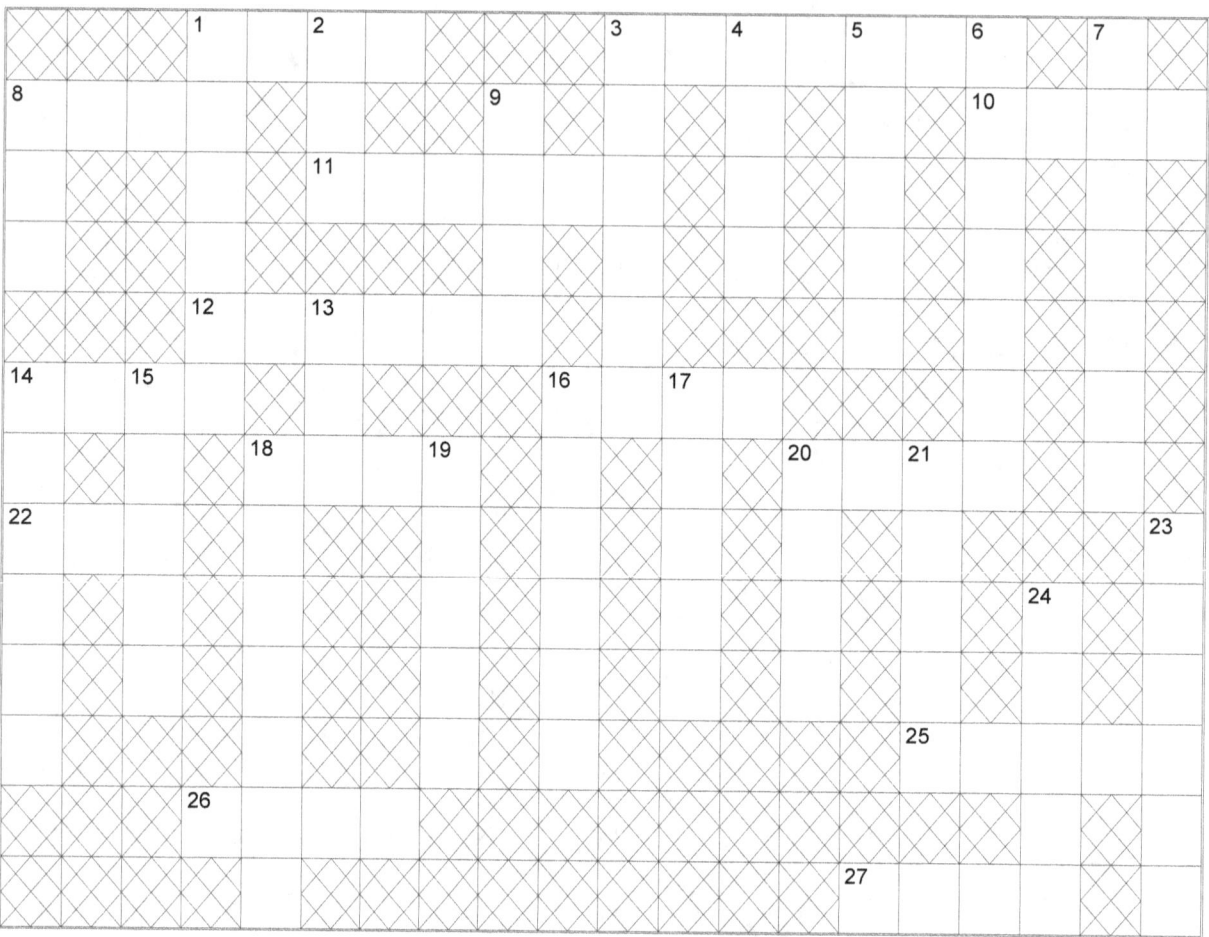

Across
1. The knight had one ____ and one day to find an answer
3. Emily's brother-in-law; he captured two knights
8. Number of husbands the Wife of Bath had
10. It branded Nicholas
11. Football-player build, cheated customers, plays bagpipes
12. Carpenter's wife
14. He tricked the miller's wife into sleeping with him
16. The older youths planned to do this to the youngest upon his return
18. The monk took this from the boy's mouth
20. The merchant's wife asked for one from Sir John
22. Pertelote, for example
25. The knight's old woman wife became ____ and beautiful
26. What the miller's wife made from the flour he took from A & J
27. Had sores, master chef

Down
1. Squire's servant
2. Carpenter broke his when he fell
3. The boy's was cut
4. Chanticleer closed his when he began to sing
5. The queen's sister; two knights loved her
6. The miller
7. She missed Arveragus
8. It came to kill Chanticleer
9. He slept with the miller's daughter
13. Anger
14. The fifth husband of the Wife of Bath
15. Arveragus tried to help save Dorigen's
16. Fiends take different ones to catch their prey
17. Place where they took the singing boy
18. Good navigator, didn't ride well, from Dartmouth
19. Griselda was beautiful in looks and ____
20. The Wife of Bath married Johnny for this, not money
21. Place where the singing boy was attacked
23. Had been in many battles, was a gentleman
24. Condition of the Miller as he told his tale

The Canterbury Tales Crossword 3 Answer Key

	1	2			3	4	5	6	7
	Y	E	A	R	T	H	E	S	E	U	S		D
8				9					10		
F	I	V	E	R		A		H	Y	M	I	R	O	N
O		O		11 M	I	L	L	E	R	E	I	M	R
X		M				A		O	S	L	P	I
		12 A	13 L	I	S	O	N	A		Y	K	G
14 J	O	15 H	N		R		16 S	17 T	A	B		I		E
O		O	18 S	E	19 E	D		H		B	20 L	21 O	A	N		N
22 H	E	N		H		E		A		B	O	L			23 K
N		O		I		E		P		E	V	L	24 D	N
N		R		P		D		E		Y	E	E	R	I
Y				M		S		E				25 Y	O	U	N	G
		26 C	A	K	E								N	H
		N								27 C	O	O	K	T

Across
1. The knight had one ____ and one day to find an answer
3. Emily's brother-in-law; he captured two knights
8. Number of husbands the Wife of Bath had
10. It branded Nicholas
11. Football-player build, cheated customers, plays bagpipes
12. Carpenter's wife
14. He tricked the miller's wife into sleeping with him
16. The older youths planned to do this to the youngest upon his return
18. The monk took this from the boy's mouth
20. The merchant's wife asked for one from Sir John
22. Pertelote, for example
25. The knight's old woman wife became ____ and beautiful
26. What the miller's wife made from the flour he took from A & J
27. Had sores, master chef

Down
1. Squire's servant
2. Carpenter broke his when he fell
3. The boy's was cut
4. Chanticleer closed his when he began to sing
5. The queen's sister; two knights loved her
6. The miller
7. She missed Arveragus
8. It came to kill Chanticleer
9. He slept with the miller's daughter
13. Anger
14. The fifth husband of the Wife of Bath
15. Arveragus tried to help save Dorigen's
16. Fiends take different ones to catch their prey
17. Place where they took the singing boy
18. Good navigator, didn't ride well, from Dartmouth
19. Griselda was beautiful in looks and ____
20. The Wife of Bath married Johnny for this, not money
21. Place where the singing boy was attacked
23. Had been in many battles, was a gentleman
24. Condition of the Miller as he told his tale

The Canterbury Tales Crossword 4

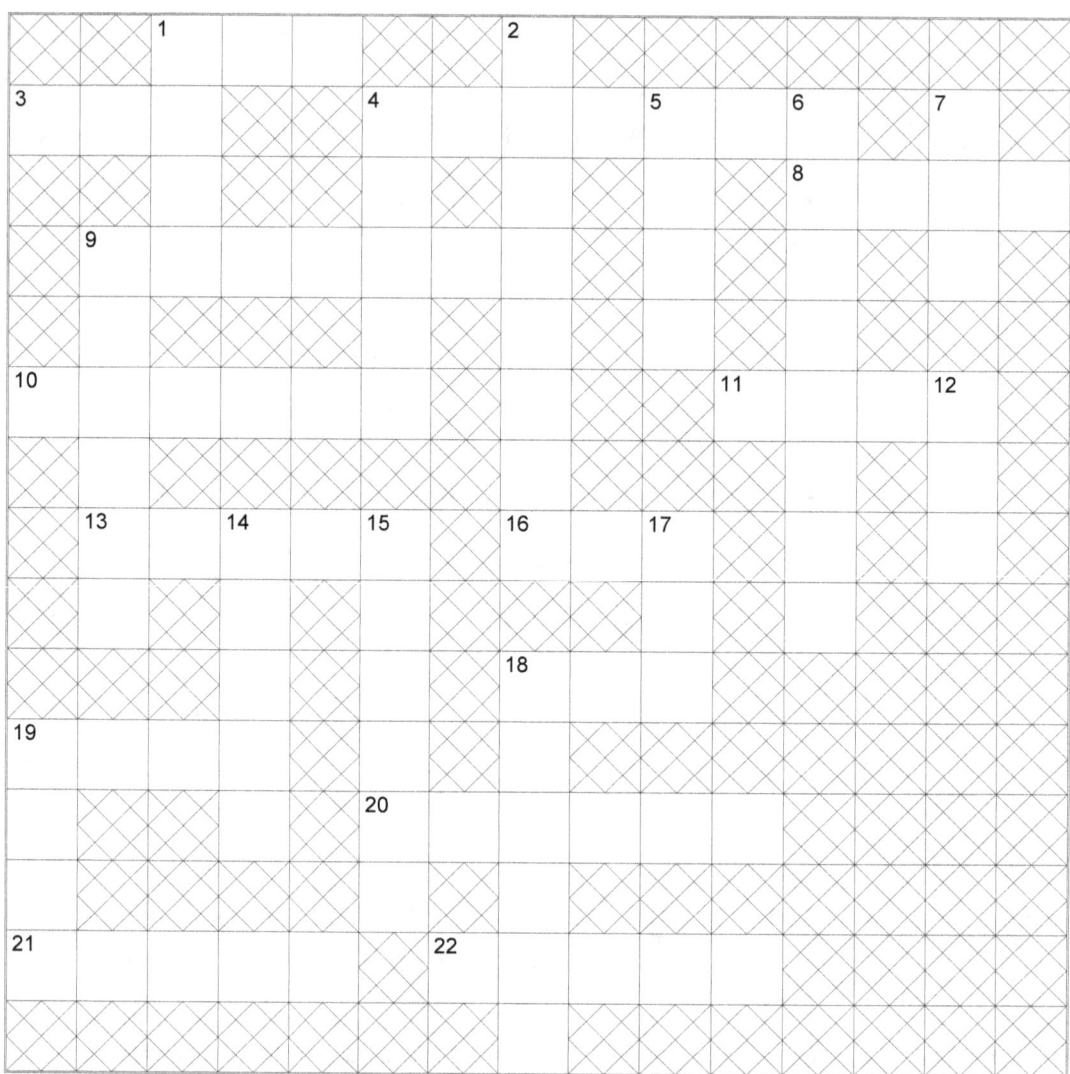

Across
1. Arcita fell onto his and broke his breast
3. Arveragus's castle was near the ____
4. She missed Arveragus
8. It branded Nicholas
9. Emily's brother-in-law; he captured two knights
10. The loan amount: 100 ____
11. He tricked the miller's wife into sleeping with him
13. Place where they took the singing boy
16. Carpenter broke his when he fell
18. He sang
19. The older youths planned to do this to the youngest upon his return
20. Carpenter's wife
21. Condition of the Miller as he told his tale
22. Place where the singing boy was attacked

Down
1. Wife of ____
2. Marquis' new wife
4. Griselda was beautiful in looks and ____
5. It was under the tree
6. Student boarder with Alison and the carpenter
7. It came to kill Chanticleer
9. The boy's was cut
12. ____'s Priest's Tale
14. Money paid to the summoner to keep him from making an arrest
15. Squire's servant
17. January's wife
18. Host
19. The monk took this from the boy's mouth

The Canterbury Tales Crossword 4 Answer Key

			1 B	O	W			2 G				
3 S	E	A		4 D	O	R	I	G	5 E	6 N		7 F
		T		E			I	O		8 I	R	O	N
	9 T	H	E	S	E	U	S		L		C		X
		H		D			E		D		H		
10 F	R	A	N	C	S		L			11 J	O	H	12 N
		O					D				L		U
	13 A	14 B	B	15 E	Y		16 A	R	17 M		A		N
		T		R					A		S		
		I		O		18 B	O	Y					
19 S	T	A	B		M		A						
		E		20 A	L	I	S	O	N				
E				N			L						
21 D	R	U	N	K		22 A	L	L	E	Y			
						Y							

Across
1. Arcita fell onto his and broke his breast
3. Arveragus's castle was near the ____
4. She missed Arveragus
8. It branded Nicholas
9. Emily's brother-in-law; he captured two knights
10. The loan amount: 100 ____
11. He tricked the miller's wife into sleeping with him
13. Place where they took the singing boy
16. Carpenter broke his when he fell
18. He sang
19. The older youths planned to do this to the youngest upon his return
20. Carpenter's wife
21. Condition of the Miller as he told his tale
22. Place where the singing boy was attacked

Down
1. Wife of ____
2. Marquis' new wife
4. Griselda was beautiful in looks and ____
5. It was under the tree
6. Student boarder with Alison and the carpenter
7. It came to kill Chanticleer
9. The boy's was cut
12. ____'s Priest's Tale
14. Money paid to the summoner to keep him from making an arrest
15. Squire's servant
17. January's wife
18. Host
19. The monk took this from the boy's mouth

The Canterbury Tales

YOUNG	BED	ABSALOM	EMILY	BRIBE
COOK	PROLOGUE	STAB	FAITH	NUN
ABBEY	JOHNNY	FREE SPACE	PARDONER	NICHOLAS
FRANCS	HONOR	BOY	FRIAR	MOLLY
DIED	SEA	ARVERAGUS	FIEND	THESEUS

The Canterbury Tales

PRAYER	KNIGHT	MILLER	YEAR	PRIORESS
SHIPMAN	GOLD	MONK	SEED	FIVE
CHANTICLEER	PALAMON	FREE SPACE	CAKE	EYES
JOHN	CHILDREN	SIMPKIN	ALISON	CLOTHES
BOW	ALLEY	CLERK	PEAR	MONEY

The Canterbury Tales

BAILLY	MAY	DIED	STAB	IRE
FIEND	ARM	CAKE	ABSALOM	SHIPMAN
FRIAR	CURSE	FREE SPACE	EMILY	IRON
TOWER	SUMMONER	ALAN	CHAUCER	DRUNK
LOVE	MILLER	PRAYER	PRIORESS	DORIGEN

The Canterbury Tales

FOX	PEAR	NICHOLAS	DEEDS	ARVERAGUS
MONK	FAITH	RELICS	BED	KNIGHT
FRANKLIN	GOLD	FREE SPACE	MONEY	ARCITA
PROLOGUE	BOY	DESIRE	WHEEL	PARSON
BRIBE	NUN	CLOTHES	KISS	HEN

The Canterbury Tales

KNIGHT	CHANTICLEER	STAB	COOK	GAS
SHAPES	PEAR	CAKE	SHIPMAN	BATH
FIEND	ABBEY	FREE SPACE	FIVE	MONEY
ARM	MERCHANT	MASTERY	SMITH	FRANCS
PARSON	SQUIRE	DEEDS	PRIORESS	JOHN

The Canterbury Tales

WHEEL	BED	EYES	NUN	TOWER
YOUNG	PROLOGUE	ABSALOM	DIED	GRISELDA
SEED	FRIAR	FREE SPACE	LOAN	DAMIAN
MONK	CLOTHES	DORIGEN	SEA	SUMMONER
DRUNK	CHILDREN	MILLER	YEOMAN	HEN

The Canterbury Tales

CHANTICLEER	THROAT	ABBEY	DORIGEN	TWO
HEN	NUN	FRANCS	MOLLY	ALLEY
GAS	TAIL	FREE SPACE	GRISELDA	MILLER
MASTERY	FOX	CHILDREN	SUMMONER	SHIPMAN
DAMIAN	DRUNK	IRON	SIMPKIN	PALAMON

The Canterbury Tales

TUBS	ALAN	EMILY	ARM	PROLOGUE
AURELIUS	EYES	SQUIRE	SMITH	SEA
DEEDS	SEED	FREE SPACE	YEOMAN	ALISON
MAY	MONK	IRE	FIEND	BED
KISS	TOWER	ADULTERY	ARCITA	PARSON

The Canterbury Tales

DEEDS	NICHOLAS	CURSE	PARDONER	PRAYER
CHAUCER	MILLER	SQUIRE	KISS	IRE
WHEEL	BOW	FREE SPACE	THESEUS	CHILDREN
EYES	PARSON	MONEY	FAITH	FRANCS
LOVE	MAY	BAILLY	ALLEY	PALAMON

The Canterbury Tales

EMILY	DRUNK	HONOR	SEA	LOAN
BED	JOHNNY	YEAR	MERCHANT	YEOMAN
ADULTERY	ARCITA	FREE SPACE	TUBS	STAB
HEN	GOLD	SHIPMAN	CLOTHES	NUN
SEED	PEAR	RELICS	ALISON	SUMMONER

The Canterbury Tales

PARSON	AURELIUS	TAIL	SUMMONER	MAY
CLERK	WHEEL	THESEUS	ABBEY	DAMIAN
SHIPMAN	MONK	FREE SPACE	HEN	REEVE
KISS	DORIGEN	BRIBE	MOLLY	FRIAR
STAB	COOK	GOLD	ALLEY	DEEDS

The Canterbury Tales

ARVERAGUS	BOY	YOUNG	FRANCS	GRISELDA
ARCITA	IRE	BATH	SQUIRE	BAILLY
IRON	CLOTHES	FREE SPACE	JOHNNY	NUN
DRUNK	JOHN	ABSALOM	TUBS	PRAYER
ARM	GAS	SEA	BED	CHANTICLEER

The Canterbury Tales

KISS	MERCHANT	FOX	RELICS	JOHNNY
SMITH	MONEY	MOLLY	CHANTICLEER	ALISON
GAS	ARVERAGUS	FREE SPACE	DORIGEN	FRANCS
ABBEY	SUMMONER	BRIBE	PARDONER	SEA
TUBS	GRISELDA	SIMPKIN	WHEEL	GOLD

The Canterbury Tales

FRANKLIN	PALAMON	THROAT	SEED	TOWER
SQUIRE	PARSON	FAITH	IRON	YOUNG
TWO	CHILDREN	FREE SPACE	LOVE	FIEND
CLERK	ARCITA	BED	ARM	ALAN
SHAPES	COOK	BAILLY	AURELIUS	YEAR

The Canterbury Tales

FIEND	JOHNNY	HONOR	PALAMON	SHIPMAN
FIVE	FRIAR	BRIBE	SMITH	ABSALOM
YEAR	CLOTHES	FREE SPACE	IRON	PRAYER
ADULTERY	CHANTICLEER	MAY	BATH	FRANKLIN
FOX	STAB	ALISON	CURSE	YOUNG

The Canterbury Tales

MASTERY	CLERK	MOLLY	DRUNK	PARSON
MERCHANT	RELICS	SEA	PEAR	ALAN
KISS	KNIGHT	FREE SPACE	JOHN	BOY
SQUIRE	ARVERAGUS	AURELIUS	LOVE	IRE
DIED	NUN	NICHOLAS	ALLEY	CHILDREN

The Canterbury Tales

EMILY	MERCHANT	STAB	GRISELDA	PARSON
JOHNNY	RELICS	BATH	YOUNG	SEA
SHAPES	MASTERY	FREE SPACE	COOK	DIED
DEEDS	CHILDREN	KNIGHT	FRANKLIN	GAS
ALAN	PARDONER	IRE	DORIGEN	YEAR

The Canterbury Tales

SUMMONER	BOW	MILLER	THROAT	TOWER
TUBS	SHIPMAN	THESEUS	PALAMON	ABSALOM
MOLLY	CHANTICLEER	FREE SPACE	EYES	MONEY
FIVE	SIMPKIN	FAITH	PRIORESS	BOY
ADULTERY	LOAN	DAMIAN	ALLEY	DESIRE

The Canterbury Tales

TAIL	DORIGEN	ABSALOM	ALISON	EMILY
SQUIRE	FRANCS	KISS	IRE	THROAT
PALAMON	BED	FREE SPACE	PRAYER	MONK
SHIPMAN	GRISELDA	CHAUCER	AURELIUS	CLOTHES
BAILLY	KNIGHT	ALAN	BATH	RELICS

The Canterbury Tales

SHAPES	JOHNNY	MERCHANT	TWO	MONEY
SUMMONER	DAMIAN	SIMPKIN	BRIBE	NICHOLAS
FIEND	WHEEL	FREE SPACE	HEN	MILLER
DIED	FRANKLIN	MOLLY	REEVE	SEA
ARVERAGUS	DRUNK	PEAR	JOHN	YOUNG

The Canterbury Tales

COOK	NICHOLAS	CAKE	EYES	ARVERAGUS
SEA	PARDONER	FOX	FIVE	DIED
SHIPMAN	SHAPES	FREE SPACE	MERCHANT	THESEUS
PRIORESS	TUBS	FIEND	BED	BOW
ARM	WHEEL	PEAR	PALAMON	MONK

The Canterbury Tales

YOUNG	PARSON	GAS	MOLLY	BAILLY
AURELIUS	IRE	GOLD	JOHNNY	SEED
ABSALOM	FRANKLIN	FREE SPACE	IRON	ALLEY
ADULTERY	ARCITA	ALISON	SQUIRE	PROLOGUE
SUMMONER	ALAN	YEAR	SMITH	DEEDS

The Canterbury Tales

SMITH	COOK	IRON	ABSALOM	WHEEL
ARCITA	GAS	THROAT	BED	SUMMONER
BRIBE	MONEY	FREE SPACE	GOLD	DRUNK
JOHNNY	TOWER	KNIGHT	YOUNG	DIED
EYES	PARDONER	YEAR	DORIGEN	ARVERAGUS

The Canterbury Tales

KISS	PEAR	BOW	SEED	LOVE
ALLEY	PARSON	REEVE	SQUIRE	FAITH
STAB	JOHN	FREE SPACE	SEA	SIMPKIN
FRANCS	PROLOGUE	AURELIUS	EMILY	ALISON
CLERK	IRE	MASTERY	LOAN	NUN

The Canterbury Tales

JOHNNY	PARSON	GRISELDA	ALISON	FRANKLIN
TAIL	SHAPES	MASTERY	PARDONER	EMILY
BAILLY	BED	FREE SPACE	PALAMON	YEOMAN
ARVERAGUS	TWO	LOVE	BATH	HONOR
CAKE	FIVE	COOK	SMITH	MILLER

The Canterbury Tales

PEAR	MONEY	ARM	TUBS	MOLLY
BOW	FOX	ABBEY	FRANCS	ABSALOM
NICHOLAS	CHAUCER	FREE SPACE	TOWER	SEED
FIEND	IRON	WHEEL	SIMPKIN	DESIRE
KNIGHT	JOHN	SHIPMAN	DRUNK	ARCITA

The Canterbury Tales

SIMPKIN	WHEEL	ADULTERY	MASTERY	THESEUS
GOLD	PROLOGUE	MOLLY	IRE	DORIGEN
RELICS	TWO	FREE SPACE	SEA	SMITH
PEAR	EMILY	PRAYER	IRON	SEED
CHAUCER	CHANTICLEER	SUMMONER	PARSON	MONEY

The Canterbury Tales

FAITH	TOWER	NICHOLAS	BED	FRANKLIN
MERCHANT	PRIORESS	BOY	GAS	LOAN
SQUIRE	CHILDREN	FREE SPACE	DRUNK	THROAT
BAILLY	ABBEY	CURSE	ARCITA	MAY
HEN	BRIBE	SHAPES	REEVE	MILLER

The Canterbury Tales

STAB	DESIRE	GOLD	SQUIRE	MAY
BED	ABBEY	EMILY	JOHNNY	SEED
GRISELDA	LOVE	FREE SPACE	SHIPMAN	FRANCS
SEA	ARM	KISS	MONK	RELICS
JOHN	FRANKLIN	ABSALOM	EYES	DRUNK

The Canterbury Tales

CAKE	HONOR	PRAYER	FRIAR	THESEUS
ADULTERY	TOWER	CHILDREN	COOK	ALLEY
BRIBE	PALAMON	FREE SPACE	BATH	ARCITA
CLOTHES	MONEY	IRE	WHEEL	BOY
YEOMAN	CHAUCER	TWO	CURSE	THROAT

The Canterbury Tales

TUBS	GAS	TOWER	FAITH	YEOMAN
PALAMON	BAILLY	ARM	SIMPKIN	TAIL
SMITH	IRE	FREE SPACE	DIED	SHIPMAN
HONOR	BRIBE	MILLER	AURELIUS	DEEDS
LOVE	NUN	ALAN	CHILDREN	DESIRE

The Canterbury Tales

MOLLY	CHAUCER	PARDONER	ADULTERY	CLOTHES
BATH	EYES	CLERK	EMILY	FOX
SHAPES	ABBEY	FREE SPACE	KISS	CAKE
FRANKLIN	LOAN	ARCITA	ALLEY	DAMIAN
GRISELDA	ABSALOM	THROAT	MONK	FIVE

Canterbury Tales Vocabulary Word List

No. Word	Clue/Definition
1. ABOMINABLE	Hateful; horrid; awful
2. ACQUIESCE	Agree; consent
3. ACQUITTAL	To free from a charge or accusation
4. AMISS	Wrong; awry
5. APHRODISIAC	A drug or food having the effect of arousing sexual desire
6. AVAIL	Usefulness
7. BENIGN	Kindhearted, considerate
8. BEQUEATH	To leave material goods by will
9. BESEECH	Make an earnest request
10. BLITHELY	Lightheartedly; festively; merrily
11. CAPRICES	Whims
12. CAROUSES	Behaves riotously; revels
13. CHIDE	To criticize for a fault or offense
14. CONSTANCY	Faithfulness; fidelity
15. CONTRIVE	Plan
16. CONUNDRUM	A mystery; a puzzle
17. COY	Given to flirting
18. DAIS	A raised platform
19. DAUNTED	Deprived of courage as a result of fear, anxiety or disgust
20. DEMURE	Reserved in manner; shy; modest
21. DERISION	Mockery; ridicule
22. DILIGENCE	Steady attention and effort
23. DISCREET	Diplomatic; politic; tactful
24. EMINENT	Widely known; famous
25. ENTHRALLED	Enchanted; fascinated
26. ESCHEW	To stay away from
27. EXHORTATION	Speech that incites
28. EXTORT	To obtain from another by intimidation or blackmail
29. FEIGNED	Artificial; counterfeited; faked
30. FELICITY	Happiness; bliss
31. FRUGALITY	Thriftiness; careful use of material goods
32. GLUTTONY	The vice of continually overeating
33. INCITING	Stirring to action
34. INEBRIATE	Drunk
35. INSINUATION	Innuendoes; indirect hints; implications
36. IRE	Anger
37. LANGUISHING	Lacking energy or strength
38. LECHER	A man who overindulges in sexual activities
39. OBSCURE	Not readily noticed or seen; unknown
40. OBSTINATE	Stubborn
41. PALLOR	Extreme paleness
42. PARAMOURS	Lovers
43. PELF	Loot; goods seized unlawfully
44. PRATING	Chattering; jabbering
45. PREDESTINATION	Belief that one's fate is already decided
46. PREROGATIVE	The right to command or decide
47. PRODIGIOUS	Of extraordinary size and/or power
48. PROFFERING	To put before another for acceptance
49. REDRESSED	To get revenge for
50. REPLETION	Full to or beyond satisfaction
51. REPREHENSIBLE	Deserving condemnation; despicable

Canterbury Tales Vocabulary Word List

No.	Word	Clue/Definition
52.	REQUITE	Repay
53.	RETINUE	Group of attendants or followers
54.	REVEL	To behave festively; frolic
55.	SAGE	Wise; wise person; scholarly
56.	SUNDRY	Consisting of many different kinds
57.	SUPPLICATIONS	Appeals; pleas
58.	TRENCHANT	Sharp
59.	USURY	Lending money & charging outrageously high interest
60.	VERILY	Even; indeed
61.	VICTUALS	Food for humans
62.	WOE	A cause of suffering or harm

Canterbury Tales Vocabulary Fill In The Blank 1

_____ 1. Repay

_____ 2. Reserved in manner; shy; modest

_____ 3. To free from a charge or accusation

_____ 4. Full to or beyond satisfaction

_____ 5. Stirring to action

_____ 6. Lovers

_____ 7. Deserving condemnation; despicable

_____ 8. Given to flirting

_____ 9. Extreme paleness

_____ 10. Hateful; horrid; awful

_____ 11. Deprived of courage as a result of fear, anxiety or disgust

_____ 12. To put before another for acceptance

_____ 13. Thriftiness; careful use of material goods

_____ 14. Loot; goods seized unlawfully

_____ 15. The vice of continually overeating

_____ 16. Group of attendants or followers

_____ 17. Steady attention and effort

_____ 18. To behave festively; frolic

_____ 19. Lightheartedly; festively; merrily

_____ 20. A drug or food having the effect of arousing sexual desire

Canterbury Tales Vocabulary Fill In The Blank 1 Answer Key

REQUITE	1. Repay
DEMURE	2. Reserved in manner; shy; modest
ACQUITTAL	3. To free from a charge or accusation
REPLETION	4. Full to or beyond satisfaction
INCITING	5. Stirring to action
PARAMOURS	6. Lovers
REPREHENSIBLE	7. Deserving condemnation; despicable
COY	8. Given to flirting
PALLOR	9. Extreme paleness
ABOMINABLE	10. Hateful; horrid; awful
DAUNTED	11. Deprived of courage as a result of fear, anxiety or disgust
PROFFERING	12. To put before another for acceptance
FRUGALITY	13. Thriftiness; careful use of material goods
PELF	14. Loot; goods seized unlawfully
GLUTTONY	15. The vice of continually overeating
RETINUE	16. Group of attendants or followers
DILIGENCE	17. Steady attention and effort
REVEL	18. To behave festively; frolic
BLITHELY	19. Lightheartedly; festively; merrily
APHRODISIAC	20. A drug or food having the effect of arousing sexual desire

Canterbury Tales Vocabulary Fill In The Blank 2

_____ 1. Make an earnest request

_____ 2. Chattering; jabbering

_____ 3. The vice of continually overeating

_____ 4. A drug or food having the effect of arousing sexual desire

_____ 5. To stay away from

_____ 6. Sharp

_____ 7. Behaves riotously; revels

_____ 8. Repay

_____ 9. Widely known; famous

_____ 10. Happiness; bliss

_____ 11. The right to command or decide

_____ 12. Plan

_____ 13. Deserving condemnation; despicable

_____ 14. Kindhearted, considerate

_____ 15. A raised platform

_____ 16. Given to flirting

_____ 17. A mystery; a puzzle

_____ 18. Wise; wise person; scholarly

_____ 19. Full to or beyond satisfaction

_____ 20. Usefulness

Canterbury Tales Vocabulary Fill In The Blank 2 Answer Key

BESEECH	1. Make an earnest request
PRATING	2. Chattering; jabbering
GLUTTONY	3. The vice of continually overeating
APHRODISIAC	4. A drug or food having the effect of arousing sexual desire
ESCHEW	5. To stay away from
TRENCHANT	6. Sharp
CAROUSES	7. Behaves riotously; revels
REQUITE	8. Repay
EMINENT	9. Widely known; famous
FELICITY	10. Happiness; bliss
PREROGATIVE	11. The right to command or decide
CONTRIVE	12. Plan
REPREHENSIBLE	13. Deserving condemnation; despicable
BENIGN	14. Kindhearted, considerate
DAIS	15. A raised platform
COY	16. Given to flirting
CONUNDRUM	17. A mystery; a puzzle
SAGE	18. Wise; wise person; scholarly
REPLETION	19. Full to or beyond satisfaction
AVAIL	20. Usefulness

Canterbury Tales Vocabulary Fill In The Blank 3

1. Extreme paleness
2. A man who overindulges in sexual activities
3. Lovers
4. Lending money & charging outrageously high interest
5. Deprived of courage as a result of fear, anxiety or disgust
6. Speech that incites
7. Behaves riotously; revels
8. Enchanted; fascinated
9. Artificial; counterfeited; faked
10. A drug or food having the effect of arousing sexual desire
11. Drunk
12. Reserved in manner; shy; modest
13. A raised platform
14. To stay away from
15. Group of attendants or followers
16. Stubborn
17. Consisting of many different kinds
18. Food for humans
19. To criticize for a fault or offense
20. Innuendoes; indirect hints; implications

Canterbury Tales Vocabulary Fill In The Blank 3 Answer Key

PALLOR	1. Extreme paleness
LECHER	2. A man who overindulges in sexual activities
PARAMOURS	3. Lovers
USURY	4. Lending money & charging outrageously high interest
DAUNTED	5. Deprived of courage as a result of fear, anxiety or disgust
EXHORTATION	6. Speech that incites
CAROUSES	7. Behaves riotously; revels
ENTHRALLED	8. Enchanted; fascinated
FEIGNED	9. Artificial; counterfeited; faked
APHRODISIAC	10. A drug or food having the effect of arousing sexual desire
INEBRIATE	11. Drunk
DEMURE	12. Reserved in manner; shy; modest
DAIS	13. A raised platform
ESCHEW	14. To stay away from
RETINUE	15. Group of attendants or followers
OBSTINATE	16. Stubborn
SUNDRY	17. Consisting of many different kinds
VICTUALS	18. Food for humans
CHIDE	19. To criticize for a fault or offense
INSINUATION	20. Innuendoes; indirect hints; implications

Canterbury Tales Vocabulary Fill In The Blank 4

_____ 1. Diplomatic; politic; tactful

_____ 2. Chattering; jabbering

_____ 3. Repay

_____ 4. A mystery; a puzzle

_____ 5. Stubborn

_____ 6. To leave material goods by will

_____ 7. Not readily noticed or seen; unknown

_____ 8. Group of attendants or followers

_____ 9. To obtain from another by intimidation or blackmail

_____ 10. Extreme paleness

_____ 11. Lacking energy or strength

_____ 12. Lending money & charging outrageously high interest

_____ 13. Belief that one's fate is already decided

_____ 14. Deprived of courage as a result of fear, anxiety or disgust

_____ 15. The vice of continually overeating

_____ 16. To free from a charge or accusation

_____ 17. Usefulness

_____ 18. Drunk

_____ 19. A man who overindulges in sexual activities

_____ 20. Deserving condemnation; despicable

Canterbury Tales Vocabulary Fill In The Blank 4 Answer Key

DISCREET	1. Diplomatic; politic; tactful
PRATING	2. Chattering; jabbering
REQUITE	3. Repay
CONUNDRUM	4. A mystery; a puzzle
OBSTINATE	5. Stubborn
BEQUEATH	6. To leave material goods by will
OBSCURE	7. Not readily noticed or seen; unknown
RETINUE	8. Group of attendants or followers
EXTORT	9. To obtain from another by intimidation or blackmail
PALLOR	10. Extreme paleness
LANGUISHING	11. Lacking energy or strength
USURY	12. Lending money & charging outrageously high interest
PREDESTINATION	13. Belief that one's fate is already decided
DAUNTED	14. Deprived of courage as a result of fear, anxiety or disgust
GLUTTONY	15. The vice of continually overeating
ACQUITTAL	16. To free from a charge or accusation
AVAIL	17. Usefulness
INEBRIATE	18. Drunk
LECHER	19. A man who overindulges in sexual activities
REPREHENSIBLE	20. Deserving condemnation; despicable

Canterbury Tales Vocabulary Matching 1

___ 1. APHRODISIAC	A. Agree; consent
___ 2. REPREHENSIBLE	B. Food for humans
___ 3. TRENCHANT	C. Given to flirting
___ 4. SUPPLICATIONS	D. Faithfulness; fidelity
___ 5. USURY	E. Appeals; pleas
___ 6. ACQUIESCE	F. A mystery; a puzzle
___ 7. EXTORT	G. To free from a charge or accusation
___ 8. CONUNDRUM	H. Happiness; bliss
___ 9. REPLETION	I. Deserving condemnation; despicable
___10. DERISION	J. Mockery; ridicule
___11. CONSTANCY	K. Wrong; awry
___12. DAIS	L. A raised platform
___13. INEBRIATE	M. Sharp
___14. DAUNTED	N. To get revenge for
___15. COY	O. To obtain from another by intimidation or blackmail
___16. REDRESSED	P. Full to or beyond satisfaction
___17. FELICITY	Q. Make an earnest request
___18. ACQUITTAL	R. Drunk
___19. ENTHRALLED	S. Enchanted; fascinated
___20. AMISS	T. Hateful; horrid; awful
___21. BLITHELY	U. Lightheartedly; festively; merrily
___22. ABOMINABLE	V. Lending money & charging outrageously high interest
___23. VICTUALS	W. A drug or food having the effect of arousing sexual desire
___24. INCITING	X. Deprived of courage as a result of fear, anxiety or disgust
___25. BESEECH	Y. Stirring to action

Canterbury Tales Vocabulary Matching 1 Answer Key

W - 1. APHRODISIAC	A. Agree; consent
I - 2. REPREHENSIBLE	B. Food for humans
M - 3. TRENCHANT	C. Given to flirting
E - 4. SUPPLICATIONS	D. Faithfulness; fidelity
V - 5. USURY	E. Appeals; pleas
A - 6. ACQUIESCE	F. A mystery; a puzzle
O - 7. EXTORT	G. To free from a charge or accusation
F - 8. CONUNDRUM	H. Happiness; bliss
P - 9. REPLETION	I. Deserving condemnation; despicable
J - 10. DERISION	J. Mockery; ridicule
D - 11. CONSTANCY	K. Wrong; awry
L - 12. DAIS	L. A raised platform
R - 13. INEBRIATE	M. Sharp
X - 14. DAUNTED	N. To get revenge for
C - 15. COY	O. To obtain from another by intimidation or blackmail
N - 16. REDRESSED	P. Full to or beyond satisfaction
H - 17. FELICITY	Q. Make an earnest request
G - 18. ACQUITTAL	R. Drunk
S - 19. ENTHRALLED	S. Enchanted; fascinated
K - 20. AMISS	T. Hateful; horrid; awful
U - 21. BLITHELY	U. Lightheartedly; festively; merrily
T - 22. ABOMINABLE	V. Lending money & charging outrageously high interest
B - 23. VICTUALS	W. A drug or food having the effect of arousing sexual desire
Y - 24. INCITING	X. Deprived of courage as a result of fear, anxiety or disgust
Q - 25. BESEECH	Y. Stirring to action

Canterbury Tales Vocabulary Matching 2

___ 1. CAROUSES   A. Usefulness
___ 2. ENTHRALLED   B. Make an earnest request
___ 3. PELF   C. Chattering; jabbering
___ 4. CONSTANCY   D. Faithfulness; fidelity
___ 5. BEQUEATH   E. Behaves riotously; revels
___ 6. AMISS   F. Plan
___ 7. USURY   G. Speech that incites
___ 8. BESEECH   H. Lending money & charging outrageously high interest
___ 9. REPLETION   I. Kindhearted, considerate
___10. LECHER   J. Artificial; counterfeited; faked
___11. DAUNTED   K. Full to or beyond satisfaction
___12. BENIGN   L. Extreme paleness
___13. FEIGNED   M. To leave material goods by will
___14. INSINUATION   N. Wrong; awry
___15. CONTRIVE   O. Deprived of courage as a result of fear, anxiety or disgust
___16. EMINENT   P. A raised platform
___17. CONUNDRUM   Q. A man who overindulges in sexual activities
___18. AVAIL   R. Loot; goods seized unlawfully
___19. WOE   S. Widely known; famous
___20. EXHORTATION   T. Innuendoes; indirect hints; implications
___21. CHIDE   U. To criticize for a fault or offense
___22. SUPPLICATIONS   V. A mystery; a puzzle
___23. PALLOR   W. Appeals; pleas
___24. DAIS   X. A cause of suffering or harm
___25. PRATING   Y. Enchanted; fascinated

Canterbury Tales Vocabulary Matching 2 Answer Key

E - 1. CAROUSES		A. Usefulness
Y - 2. ENTHRALLED		B. Make an earnest request
R - 3. PELF		C. Chattering; jabbering
D - 4. CONSTANCY		D. Faithfulness; fidelity
M - 5. BEQUEATH		E. Behaves riotously; revels
N - 6. AMISS		F. Plan
H - 7. USURY		G. Speech that incites
B - 8. BESEECH		H. Lending money & charging outrageously high interest
K - 9. REPLETION		I. Kindhearted, considerate
Q -10. LECHER		J. Artificial; counterfeited; faked
O -11. DAUNTED		K. Full to or beyond satisfaction
I - 12. BENIGN		L. Extreme paleness
J - 13. FEIGNED		M. To leave material goods by will
T - 14. INSINUATION		N. Wrong; awry
F - 15. CONTRIVE		O. Deprived of courage as a result of fear, anxiety or disgust
S - 16. EMINENT		P. A raised platform
V - 17. CONUNDRUM		Q. A man who overindulges in sexual activities
A - 18. AVAIL		R. Loot; goods seized unlawfully
X - 19. WOE		S. Widely known; famous
G - 20. EXHORTATION		T. Innuendoes; indirect hints; implications
U - 21. CHIDE		U. To criticize for a fault or offense
W - 22. SUPPLICATIONS		V. A mystery; a puzzle
L - 23. PALLOR		W. Appeals; pleas
P - 24. DAIS		X. A cause of suffering or harm
C - 25. PRATING		Y. Enchanted; fascinated

Canterbury Tales Vocabulary Matching 3

___ 1. ENTHRALLED   A. The right to command or decide
___ 2. VERILY   B. Wise; wise person; scholarly
___ 3. GLUTTONY   C. To stay away from
___ 4. INEBRIATE   D. Not readily noticed or seen; unknown
___ 5. INCITING   E. Full to or beyond satisfaction
___ 6. PROFFERING   F. Even; indeed
___ 7. BLITHELY   G. Steady attention and effort
___ 8. OBSTINATE   H. To put before another for acceptance
___ 9. USURY   I. Lightheartedly; festively; merrily
___ 10. ABOMINABLE   J. Enchanted; fascinated
___ 11. INSINUATION   K. Make an earnest request
___ 12. ACQUIESCE   L. To criticize for a fault or offense
___ 13. SAGE   M. Drunk
___ 14. BESEECH   N. Stubborn
___ 15. TRENCHANT   O. The vice of continually overeating
___ 16. LANGUISHING   P. Agree; consent
___ 17. OBSCURE   Q. Lacking energy or strength
___ 18. ESCHEW   R. Stirring to action
___ 19. PREROGATIVE   S. Hateful; horrid; awful
___ 20. REPLETION   T. Innuendoes; indirect hints; implications
___ 21. PREDESTINATION   U. Lending money & charging outrageously high interest
___ 22. CHIDE   V. Artificial; counterfeited; faked
___ 23. DILIGENCE   W. Belief that one's fate is already decided
___ 24. FEIGNED   X. Sharp
___ 25. DEMURE   Y. Reserved in manner; shy; modest

Canterbury Tales Vocabulary Matching 3 Answer Key

J - 1. ENTHRALLED   A. The right to command or decide
F - 2. VERILY   B. Wise; wise person; scholarly
O - 3. GLUTTONY   C. To stay away from
M - 4. INEBRIATE   D. Not readily noticed or seen; unknown
R - 5. INCITING   E. Full to or beyond satisfaction
H - 6. PROFFERING   F. Even; indeed
I - 7. BLITHELY   G. Steady attention and effort
N - 8. OBSTINATE   H. To put before another for acceptance
U - 9. USURY   I. Lightheartedly; festively; merrily
S - 10. ABOMINABLE   J. Enchanted; fascinated
T - 11. INSINUATION   K. Make an earnest request
P - 12. ACQUIESCE   L. To criticize for a fault or offense
B - 13. SAGE   M. Drunk
K - 14. BESEECH   N. Stubborn
X - 15. TRENCHANT   O. The vice of continually overeating
Q - 16. LANGUISHING   P. Agree; consent
D - 17. OBSCURE   Q. Lacking energy or strength
C - 18. ESCHEW   R. Stirring to action
A - 19. PREROGATIVE   S. Hateful; horrid; awful
E - 20. REPLETION   T. Innuendoes; indirect hints; implications
W - 21. PREDESTINATION   U. Lending money & charging outrageously high interest
L - 22. CHIDE   V. Artificial; counterfeited; faked
G - 23. DILIGENCE   W. Belief that one's fate is already decided
V - 24. FEIGNED   X. Sharp
Y - 25. DEMURE   Y. Reserved in manner; shy; modest

Canterbury Tales Vocabulary Matching 4

___ 1. LECHER   A. Stirring to action
___ 2. INCITING   B. Thriftiness; careful use of material goods
___ 3. ABOMINABLE   C. To put before another for acceptance
___ 4. FEIGNED   D. Deserving condemnation; despicable
___ 5. IRE   E. Group of attendants or followers
___ 6. RETINUE   F. Given to flirting
___ 7. COY   G. Anger
___ 8. REQUITE   H. Behaves riotously; revels
___ 9. BESEECH   I. Drunk
___ 10. PREROGATIVE   J. Lightheartedly; festively; merrily
___ 11. VERILY   K. Of extraordinary size and/or power
___ 12. REDRESSED   L. The right to command or decide
___ 13. PROFFERING   M. Even; indeed
___ 14. BENIGN   N. A raised platform
___ 15. INEBRIATE   O. Steady attention and effort
___ 16. ACQUIESCE   P. To get revenge for
___ 17. VICTUALS   Q. Kindhearted, considerate
___ 18. BLITHELY   R. Repay
___ 19. DAIS   S. Agree; consent
___ 20. EXHORTATION   T. A man who overindulges in sexual activities
___ 21. DILIGENCE   U. Speech that incites
___ 22. PRODIGIOUS   V. Food fro humans
___ 23. REPREHENSIBLE   W. Artificial; counterfeited; faked
___ 24. CAROUSES   X. Make an earnest request
___ 25. FRUGALITY   Y. Hateful; horrid; awful

Canterbury Tales Vocabulary Matching 4 Answer Key

T - 1. LECHER	A.	Stirring to action
A - 2. INCITING	B.	Thriftiness; careful use of material goods
Y - 3. ABOMINABLE	C.	To put before another for acceptance
W - 4. FEIGNED	D.	Deserving condemnation; despicable
G - 5. IRE	E.	Group of attendants or followers
E - 6. RETINUE	F.	Given to flirting
F - 7. COY	G.	Anger
R - 8. REQUITE	H.	Behaves riotously; revels
X - 9. BESEECH	I.	Drunk
L - 10. PREROGATIVE	J.	Lightheartedly; festively; merrily
M - 11. VERILY	K.	Of extraordinary size and/or power
P - 12. REDRESSED	L.	The right to command or decide
C - 13. PROFFERING	M.	Even; indeed
Q - 14. BENIGN	N.	A raised platform
I - 15. INEBRIATE	O.	Steady attention and effort
S - 16. ACQUIESCE	P.	To get revenge for
V - 17. VICTUALS	Q.	Kindhearted, considerate
J - 18. BLITHELY	R.	Repay
N - 19. DAIS	S.	Agree; consent
U - 20. EXHORTATION	T.	A man who overindulges in sexual activities
O - 21. DILIGENCE	U.	Speech that incites
K - 22. PRODIGIOUS	V.	Food fro humans
D - 23. REPREHENSIBLE	W.	Artificial; counterfeited; faked
H - 24. CAROUSES	X.	Make an earnest request
B - 25. FRUGALITY	Y.	Hateful; horrid; awful

Canterbury Tales Vocabulary Magic Squares 1

Match the definition with the vocabulary word. Put your answers in the magic squares below. When your answers are correct, all columns and rows will add to the same number.

A. BLITHELY
B. CAPRICES
C. APHRODISIAC
D. FELICITY
E. DISCREET
F. LECHER
G. REPLETION
H. COY
I. REQUITE
J. PELF
K. DAIS
L. CHIDE
M. ACQUITTAL
N. WOE
O. GLUTTONY
P. FEIGNED

1. Given to flirting
2. To free from a charge or accusation
3. Whims
4. A raised platform
5. Loot; goods seized unlawfully
6. A drug or food having the effect of arousing sexual desire
7. Artificial; counterfeited; faked
8. Diplomatic; politic; tactful
9. The vice of continually overeating
10. A man who overindulges in sexual activities
11. Repay
12. Happiness; bliss
13. Lightheartedly; festively; merrily
14. To criticize for a fault or offense
15. Full to or beyond satisfaction
16. A cause of suffering or harm

A=	B=	C=	D=
E=	F=	G=	H=
I=	J=	K=	L=
M=	N=	O=	P=

Canterbury Tales Vocabulary Magic Squares 1 Answer Key

Match the definition with the vocabulary word. Put your answers in the magic squares below. When your answers are correct, all columns and rows will add to the same number.

A. BLITHELY
B. CAPRICES
C. APHRODISIAC
D. FELICITY
E. DISCREET
F. LECHER
G. REPLETION
H. COY
I. REQUITE
J. PELF
K. DAIS
L. CHIDE
M. ACQUITTAL
N. WOE
O. GLUTTONY
P. FEIGNED

1. Given to flirting
2. To free from a charge or accusation
3. Whims
4. A raised platform
5. Loot; goods seized unlawfully
6. A drug or food having the effect of arousing sexual desire
7. Artificial; counterfeited; faked
8. Diplomatic; politic; tactful
9. The vice of continually overeating
10. A man who overindulges in sexual activities
11. Repay
12. Happiness; bliss
13. Lightheartedly; festively; merrily
14. To criticize for a fault or offense
15. Full to or beyond satisfaction
16. A cause of suffering or harm

A=13	B=3	C=6	D=12
E=8	F=10	G=15	H=1
I=11	J=5	K=4	L=14
M=2	N=16	O=9	P=7

Canterbury Tales Vocabulary Magic Squares 2

Match the definition with the vocabulary word. Put your answers in the magic squares below. When your answers are correct, all columns and rows will add to the same number.

A. ENTHRALLED
B. IRE
C. WOE
D. OBSTINATE
E. DILIGENCE
F. REPLETION
G. EXHORTATION
H. INSINUATION
I. DAUNTED
J. OBSCURE
K. BEQUEATH
L. DERISION
M. REVEL
N. PREROGATIVE
O. AMISS
P. REQUITE

1. To behave festively; frolic
2. Full to or beyond satisfaction
3. Innuendoes; indirect hints; implications
4. Wrong; awry
5. Mockery; ridicule
6. A cause of suffering or harm
7. Enchanted; fascinated
8. Not readily noticed or seen; unknown
9. To leave material goods by will
10. Stubborn
11. Anger
12. Deprived of courage as a result of fear, anxiety or disgust
13. The right to command or decide
14. Steady attention and effort
15. Speech that incites
16. Repay

A=	B=	C=	D=
E=	F=	G=	H=
I=	J=	K=	L=
M=	N=	O=	P=

Canterbury Tales Vocabulary Magic Squares 2 Answer Key

Match the definition with the vocabulary word. Put your answers in the magic squares below. When your answers are correct, all columns and rows will add to the same number.

A. ENTHRALLED
B. IRE
C. WOE
D. OBSTINATE
E. DILIGENCE
F. REPLETION
G. EXHORTATION
H. INSINUATION
I. DAUNTED
J. OBSCURE
K. BEQUEATH
L. DERISION
M. REVEL
N. PREROGATIVE
O. AMISS
P. REQUITE

1. To behave festively; frolic
2. Full to or beyond satisfaction
3. Innuendoes; indirect hints; implications
4. Wrong; awry
5. Mockery; ridicule
6. A cause of suffering or harm
7. Enchanted; fascinated
8. Not readily noticed or seen; unknown
9. To leave material goods by will
10. Stubborn
11. Anger
12. Deprived of courage as a result of fear, anxiety or disgust
13. The right to command or decide
14. Steady attention and effort
15. Speech that incites
16. Repay

A=7	B=11	C=6	D=10
E=14	F=2	G=15	H=3
I=12	J=8	K=9	L=5
M=1	N=13	O=4	P=16

Canterbury Tales Vocabulary Magic Squares 3

Match the definition with the vocabulary word. Put your answers in the magic squares below. When your answers are correct, all columns and rows will add to the same number.

A. PRATING
B. INSINUATION
C. PREDESTINATION
D. INEBRIATE
E. PARAMOURS
F. WOE
G. DAUNTED
H. COY
I. CONTRIVE
J. EMINENT
K. USURY
L. CONSTANCY
M. RETINUE
N. PRODIGIOUS
O. IRE
P. GLUTTONY

1. Of extraordinary size and/or power
2. Deprived of courage as a result of fear, anxiety or disgust
3. Faithfulness; fidelity
4. Chattering; jabbering
5. Lending money & charging outrageously high interest
6. Innuendoes; indirect hints; implications
7. Group of attendants or followers
8. Given to flirting
9. Lovers
10. The vice of continually overeating
11. Belief that one's fate is already decided
12. Widely known; famous
13. Drunk
14. Plan
15. A cause of suffering or harm
16. Anger

A=	B=	C=	D=
E=	F=	G=	H=
I=	J=	K=	L=
M=	N=	O=	P=

Canterbury Tales Vocabulary Magic Squares 3 Answer Key

Match the definition with the vocabulary word. Put your answers in the magic squares below. When your answers are correct, all columns and rows will add to the same number.

A. PRATING
B. INSINUATION
C. PREDESTINATION
D. INEBRIATE
E. PARAMOURS
F. WOE
G. DAUNTED
H. COY
I. CONTRIVE
J. EMINENT
K. USURY
L. CONSTANCY
M. RETINUE
N. PRODIGIOUS
O. IRE
P. GLUTTONY

1. Of extraordinary size and/or power
2. Deprived of courage as a result of fear, anxiety or disgust
3. Faithfulness; fidelity
4. Chattering; jabbering
5. Lending money & charging outrageously high interest
6. Innuendoes; indirect hints; implications
7. Group of attendants or followers
8. Given to flirting
9. Lovers
10. The vice of continually overeating
11. Belief that one's fate is already decided
12. Widely known; famous
13. Drunk
14. Plan
15. A cause of suffering or harm
16. Anger

A=4	B=6	C=11	D=13
E=9	F=15	G=2	H=8
I=14	J=12	K=5	L=3
M=7	N=1	O=16	P=10

Canterbury Tales Vocabulary Magic Squares 4

Match the definition with the vocabulary word. Put your answers in the magic squares below. When your answers are correct, all columns and rows will add to the same number.

A. EXHORTATION
B. ESCHEW
C. REQUITE
D. USURY
E. OBSCURE
F. INEBRIATE
G. DERISION
H. CHIDE
I. PARAMOURS
J. REPREHENSIBLE
K. BENIGN
L. WOE
M. GLUTTONY
N. VICTUALS
O. DEMURE
P. SUPPLICATIONS

1. Repay
2. Deserving condemnation; despicable
3. Drunk
4. Reserved in manner; shy; modest
5. Appeals; pleas
6. Not readily noticed or seen; unknown
7. Lovers
8. Lending money & charging outrageously high interest
9. The vice of continually overeating
10. To criticize for a fault or offense
11. A cause of suffering or harm
12. Speech that incites
13. To stay away from
14. Kindhearted, considerate
15. Mockery; ridicule
16. Food for humans

A=	B=	C=	D=
E=	F=	G=	H=
I=	J=	K=	L=
M=	N=	O=	P=

Canterbury Tales Vocabulary Magic Squares 4 Answer Key

Match the definition with the vocabulary word. Put your answers in the magic squares below. When your answers are correct, all columns and rows will add to the same number.

A. EXHORTATION
B. ESCHEW
C. REQUITE
D. USURY
E. OBSCURE
F. INEBRIATE
G. DERISION
H. CHIDE
I. PARAMOURS
J. REPREHENSIBLE
K. BENIGN
L. WOE
M. GLUTTONY
N. VICTUALS
O. DEMURE
P. SUPPLICATIONS

1. Repay
2. Deserving condemnation; despicable
3. Drunk
4. Reserved in manner; shy; modest
5. Appeals; pleas
6. Not readily noticed or seen; unknown
7. Lovers
8. Lending money & charging outrageously high interest
9. The vice of continually overeating
10. To criticize for a fault or offense
11. A cause of suffering or harm
12. Speech that incites
13. To stay away from
14. Kindhearted, considerate
15. Mockery; ridicule
16. Food for humans

A=12	B=13	C=1	D=8
E=6	F=3	G=15	H=10
I=7	J=2	K=14	L=11
M=9	N=16	O=4	P=5

Canterbury Tales Vocabulary Word Search 1

```
L X E D N C B H F S U N D R Y F G R O P
N H Q M H R K X E G C J G Q M E S X B N
X C V I I C C D L P R O D I G I O U S B
N E D J G N I T I C N I N B C G X V T T
D E V F Z L E W C P P P Q U B N B K I B
V S L K V E B N I E M C T E N E R N N J
T E O W L C J D T D A U N T E D O H A W
P B R E B H P A Y H S T Y S E I R Q T X
T L V I S E I I S J H B C S S H U E V
Y E L K L R D S P R P H S I B C Q X M T
R R C B B Y F V A G E E R A T R O T X E
C I O E Z T S L Y W R E W Z G E A B G Q
A N N N V R L X W D D P B S T E M N Q N
R I T I D E A K E P R Y L E H T I L B F
O M R G D N U R R A E R J C Q T S G Y F
U P I N W C T X H L T U J I A U S S Q W
S H V R G H C X Z L I S C R S X E Q T X
E B E X Y A I W V O N U P P D Y V A J G
S H M S Z N V N L R U M H A O V X F T L
R E Q U I T E R U M E D G C A V A I L H
```

A cause of suffering or harm (3)
A man who overindulges in sexual activities (6)
A mystery; a puzzle (9)
A raised platform (4)
Anger (3)
Artificial; counterfeited; faked (7)
Behaves riotously; revels (8)
Chattering; jabbering (7)
Consisting of many different kinds (6)
Deprived of courage as a result of fear, anxiety or disgust (7)
Diplomatic; politic; tactful (8)
Drunk (9)
Enchanted; fascinated (10)
Even; indeed (6)
Extreme paleness (6)
Food for humans (8)
Given to flirting (3)
Group of attendants or followers (7)
Happiness; bliss (8)
Kindhearted, considerate (6)
Lending money & charging outrageously high interest (5)

Lightheartedly; festively; merrily (8)
Loot; goods seized unlawfully (4)
Make an earnest request (7)
Mockery; ridicule (8)
Of extraordinary size and/or power (10)
Plan (8)
Repay (7)
Reserved in manner; shy; modest (6)
Sharp (9)
Stirring to action (8)
Stubborn (9)
To behave festively; frolic (5)
To criticize for a fault or offense (5)
To get revenge for (9)
To leave material goods by will (8)
To obtain from another by intimidation or blackmail (6)
To stay away from (6)
Usefulness (5)
Whims (8)
Widely known; famous (7)
Wise; wise person; scholarly (4)
Wrong; awry (5)

Canterbury Tales Vocabulary Word Search 1 Answer Key

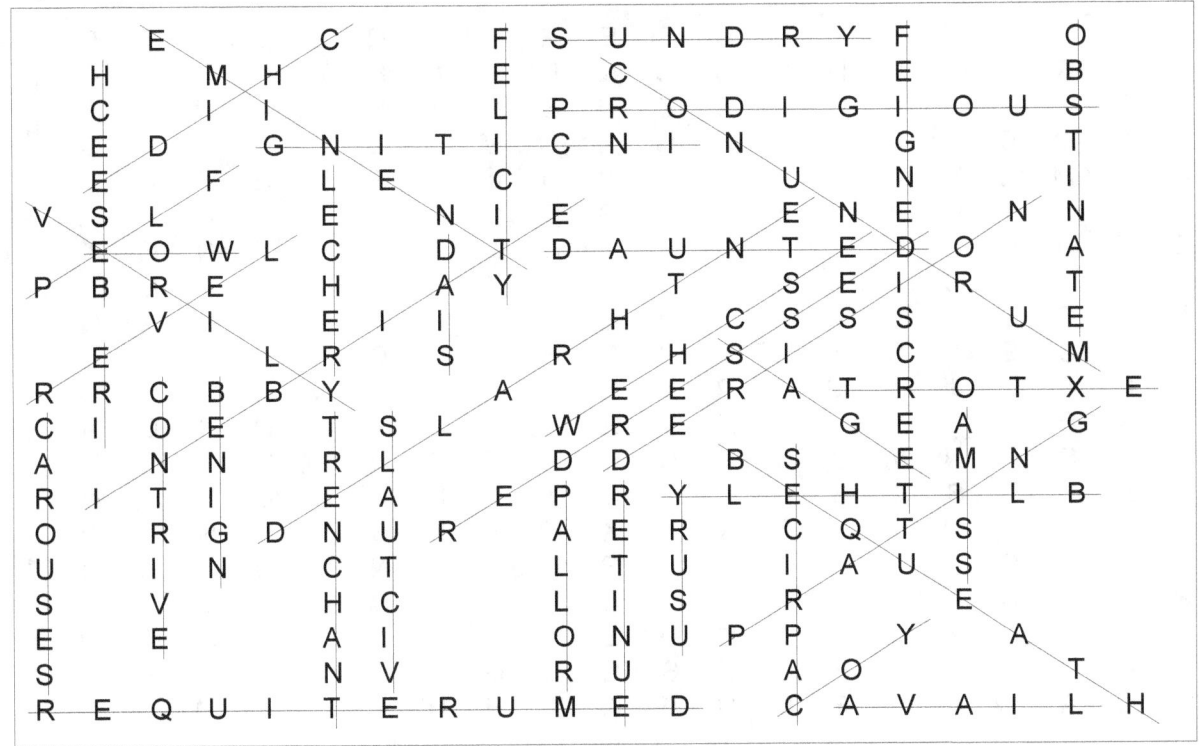

A cause of suffering or harm (3)
A man who overindulges in sexual activities (6)
A mystery; a puzzle (9)
A raised platform (4)
Anger (3)
Artificial; counterfeited; faked (7)
Behaves riotously; revels (8)
Chattering; jabbering (7)
Consisting of many different kinds (6)
Deprived of courage as a result of fear, anxiety or disgust (7)
Diplomatic; politic; tactful (8)
Drunk (9)
Enchanted; fascinated (10)
Even; indeed (6)
Extreme paleness (6)
Food for humans (8)
Given to flirting (3)
Group of attendants or followers (7)
Happiness; bliss (8)
Kindhearted, considerate (6)
Lending money & charging outrageously high interest (5)

Lightheartedly; festively; merrily (8)
Loot; goods seized unlawfully (4)
Make an earnest request (7)
Mockery; ridicule (8)
Of extraordinary size and/or power (10)
Plan (8)
Repay (7)
Reserved in manner; shy; modest (6)
Sharp (9)
Stirring to action (8)
Stubborn (9)
To behave festively; frolic (5)
To criticize for a fault or offense (5)
To get revenge for (9)
To leave material goods by will (8)
To obtain from another by intimidation or blackmail (6)
To stay away from (6)
Usefulness (5)
Whims (8)
Widely known; famous (7)
Wise; wise person; scholarly (4)
Wrong; awry (5)

Canterbury Tales Vocabulary Word Search 2

```
D A U N T E D E S S E R D E R E E G E F
N K R L X F H S U G N E L N H X M L C G
K G M T J C K O S Z N B C T N H I U S T
K Y O D E P I S F G A O M H C O N T E B
P R M E Y G L R I N N B L R E R E T I W
T X S V I A V E I T G S C A D T N O U M
S E N D U G F M R S J C M L I A T N Q T
B Z O T C C O I J U W U X L H T X Y C J
M R C B W B V X T P Z R S E C I R P A C
P I S E A E A E B P P E E D B O P O B C
V L S N J X M F R L S E H V W N D B B O
Z X E I M V I W X I R P L Y E E D S C N
Q P S G N W S M G C L E D F R L D T Z U
U A U N S C S N X A E Y T I L S E I L N
S L O D Q R I Z X T X K S I S M M N D D
U L R C E T L T I I C I Y S N C U A A R
R O A H A I S U I O O T O S M U R T I U
Y R C R A Q Q A K N E S C H E W E E S M
R E P V L E F S G S G Q D Q R O N W E F
L Q A W R B E Q U E A T H R I E K M T T
```

A cause of suffering or harm (3)
A man who overindulges in sexual activities (6)
A mystery; a puzzle (9)
A raised platform (4)
Agree; consent (9)
Anger (3)
Appeals; pleas (13)
Artificial; counterfeited; faked (7)
Behaves riotously; revels (8)
Chattering; jabbering (7)
Deprived of courage as a result of fear, anxiety or disgust (7)
Diplomatic; politic; tactful (8)
Enchanted; fascinated (10)
Even; indeed (6)
Extreme paleness (6)
Food for humans (8)
Given to flirting (3)
Group of attendants or followers (7)
Hateful; horrid; awful (10)
Kindhearted, considerate (6)
Lending money & charging outrageously high interest (5)

Loot; goods seized unlawfully (4)
Make an earnest request (7)
Mockery; ridicule (8)
Not readily noticed or seen; unknown (7)
Of extraordinary size and/or power (10)
Plan (8)
Repay (7)
Reserved in manner; shy; modest (6)
Speech that incites (11)
Stirring to action (8)
Stubborn (9)
The vice of continually overeating (8)
To behave festively; frolic (5)
To criticize for a fault or offense (5)
To get revenge for (9)
To leave material goods by will (8)
To obtain from another by intimidation or blackmail (6)
To stay away from (6)
Usefulness (5)
Whims (8)
Widely known; famous (7)
Wise; wise person; scholarly (4)
Wrong; awry (5)

Canterbury Tales Vocabulary Word Search 2 Answer Key

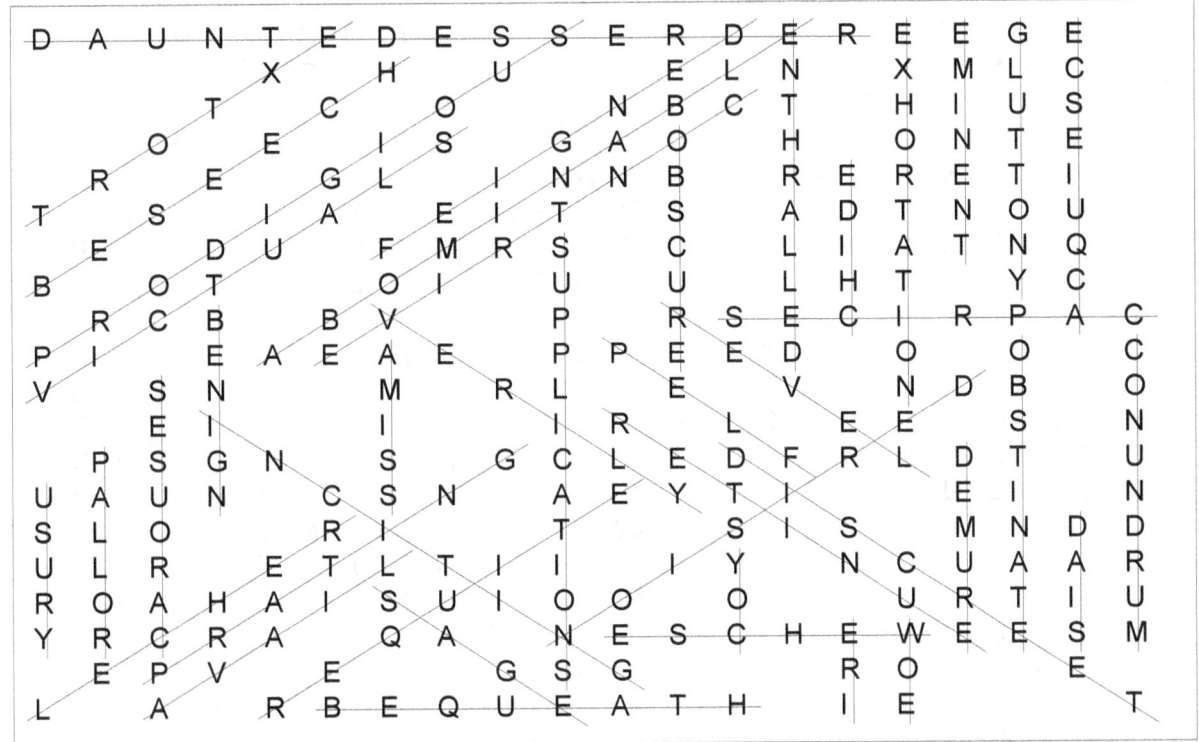

A cause of suffering or harm (3)
A man who overindulges in sexual activities (6)
A mystery; a puzzle (9)
A raised platform (4)
Agree; consent (9)
Anger (3)
Appeals; pleas (13)
Artificial; counterfeited; faked (7)
Behaves riotously; revels (8)
Chattering; jabbering (7)
Deprived of courage as a result of fear, anxiety or disgust (7)
Diplomatic; politic; tactful (8)
Enchanted; fascinated (10)
Even; indeed (6)
Extreme paleness (6)
Food for humans (8)
Given to flirting (3)
Group of attendants or followers (7)
Hateful; horrid; awful (10)
Kindhearted, considerate (6)
Lending money & charging outrageously high interest (5)

Loot; goods seized unlawfully (4)
Make an earnest request (7)
Mockery; ridicule (8)
Not readily noticed or seen; unknown (7)
Of extraordinary size and/or power (10)
Plan (8)
Repay (7)
Reserved in manner; shy; modest (6)
Speech that incites (11)
Stirring to action (8)
Stubborn (9)
The vice of continually overeating (8)
To behave festively; frolic (5)
To criticize for a fault or offense (5)
To get revenge for (9)
To leave material goods by will (8)
To obtain from another by intimidation or blackmail (6)
To stay away from (6)
Usefulness (5)
Whims (8)
Widely known; famous (7)
Wise; wise person; scholarly (4)
Wrong; awry (5)

Canterbury Tales Vocabulary Word Search 3

```
S U N D R Y E L B A N I M O B A D E N G I E F H G
S G J W N E S T F C D I L I G E N C E S T T Y C N
V C L R D V P M M Q N Z N Y M S M V B M R V X E I
D G W U Z E L L S U L C Z U I G H C N E E E H E R
Q D W J T N S B E I I K R A L B V O Y L N R D S E
S Y N O I T A N I T S E D E R P Y Y T I C I L E F
M D Y D R H O Q I T I L S O Q R A E I Y H L G B F
A R I O M R T N R A B O L N S E E R L C A Y Y N O
R V T R M A G Y Y L I L N S E R G V A V N X C C R
V X A P E L F E J N A W A E C O A P G M T H O G P
E I A I V L X R S P P O M S I G S P U Y O N N N R
O S C C L E U I E C V E I U R A Z R R B S U T I E
X B V T Q D N S K T H D S O P T P X F T H E R H D
L G S D U U O S U J I E S R A I Z R A T X M I S R
R E N T A A I B Q R Z N W A C V R N A M J I V I E
V S C T I U L E S B Y S U C Y E C E J T T N E U S
J G I H B N N S S C K G R E Y Y U X V H I E C G S
F O S K E Q A T Y C U E T I U Q E R G E G N Y N E
N T W N W R B T E H E R N H E S K D Q R L T G A D
B L I T H E L Y E D L Y E B D E R I S I O N Q L G
```

ABOMINABLE	DILIGENCE	PELF
ACQUIESCE	DISCREET	PRATING
ACQUITTAL	EMINENT	PREDESTINATION
AMISS	ENTHRALLED	PREROGATIVE
AVAIL	ESCHEW	PROFFERING
BENIGN	EXTORT	REDRESSED
BEQUEATH	FEIGNED	REPLETION
BESEECH	FELICITY	REQUITE
BLITHELY	FRUGALITY	RETINUE
CAPRICES	GLUTTONY	REVEL
CAROUSES	INCITING	SAGE
CHIDE	INSINUATION	SUNDRY
CONSTANCY	IRE	TRENCHANT
CONTRIVE	LANGUISHING	USURY
COY	LECHER	VERILY
DAIS	OBSCURE	VICTUALS
DAUNTED	OBSTINATE	WOE
DEMURE	PALLOR	
DERISION	PARAMOURS	

Canterbury Tales Vocabulary Word Search 3 Answer Key

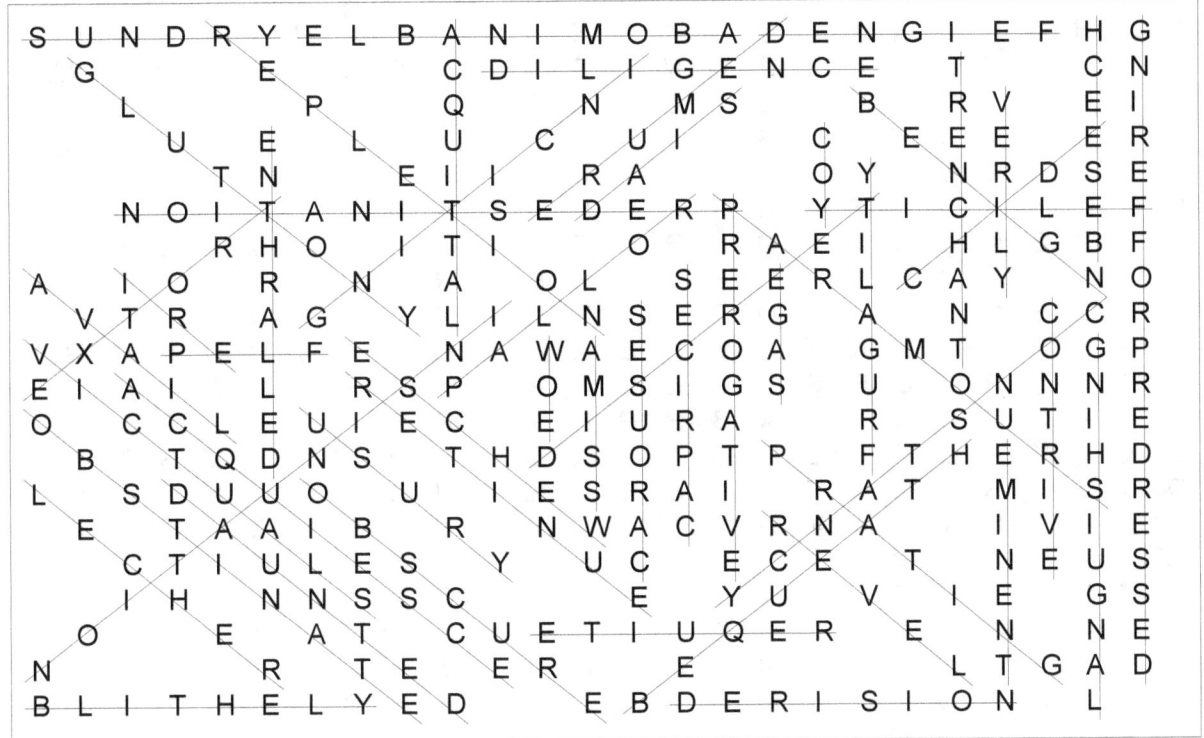

ABOMINABLE	DILIGENCE	PELF
ACQUIESCE	DISCREET	PRATING
ACQUITTAL	EMINENT	PREDESTINATION
AMISS	ENTHRALLED	PREROGATIVE
AVAIL	ESCHEW	PROFFERING
BENIGN	EXTORT	REDRESSED
BEQUEATH	FEIGNED	REPLETION
BESEECH	FELICITY	REQUITE
BLITHELY	FRUGALITY	RETINUE
CAPRICES	GLUTTONY	REVEL
CAROUSES	INCITING	SAGE
CHIDE	INSINUATION	SUNDRY
CONSTANCY	IRE	TRENCHANT
CONTRIVE	LANGUISHING	USURY
COY	LECHER	VERILY
DAIS	OBSCURE	VICTUALS
DAUNTED	OBSTINATE	WOE
DEMURE	PALLOR	
DERISION	PARAMOURS	

Canterbury Tales Vocabulary Word Search 4 Answer Key

```
E X H O R T A T I O N Y P K N O I T A U N I S N I
D I L I G E N C E B Q N H D N B Z R S F D H R S W
F V C L M P X G D E Y L R X D L T E D I T T E L G
R E R S Q A M V E S R L E W B I X N S T X M T E N
U C E A Q L J R R E D Y D C D T P C Y J B S I V I
G S Q T B L C W I E N V R W H H R H Z P L W N E H
A E U E M O O B S C U R E F L E P A R A M O U R S
L I I R M R M E I H S L S R E L R N U M V E E E I
I U T E Y I C I O D B L S T I Y Y T Q I N A S P U
T Q E J X I N K N I W R E A M L C Q Y S C U I G G
Y C T I R T S E S A W E D P R I Y J E S O D O L N
K A X P R I O N N A B P G H V O D N T R N E B U A
V X A K A E E R C T G L L R C E A D A F S M S T L
D C G D G H G Q T D N E E O M S U C I E T U T T H
Q Y H J E N U K W G I T V D K C N X R L A R I O G
W T G R I I M Z I H T I F I C H T C B I N E N N H
T M P T T H V N R V I O G S H E E N E C C N A Y L
R E A T G Q E T L C C N D I I W D W N I Y Z T K N
R R A V C B F E I G N E D A D L J R I T V C E H F
P L C O N T R I V E I M D C E Z H B C Y R X Y N Q
```

ABOMINABLE	DERISION	OBSTINATE
ACQUIESCE	DILIGENCE	PALLOR
ACQUITTAL	DISCREET	PARAMOURS
AMISS	EMINENT	PELF
APHRODISIAC	ESCHEW	PRATING
AVAIL	EXHORTATION	REDRESSED
BENIGN	EXTORT	REPLETION
BESEECH	FEIGNED	REPREHENSIBLE
BLITHELY	FELICITY	REQUITE
CAPRICES	FRUGALITY	RETINUE
CAROUSES	GLUTTONY	REVEL
CHIDE	INCITING	SAGE
CONSTANCY	INEBRIATE	SUNDRY
CONTRIVE	INSINUATION	TRENCHANT
COY	IRE	USURY
DAIS	LANGUISHING	VERILY
DAUNTED	LECHER	VICTUALS
DEMURE	OBSCURE	WOE

Canterbury Tales Vocabulary Word Search 4 Answer Key

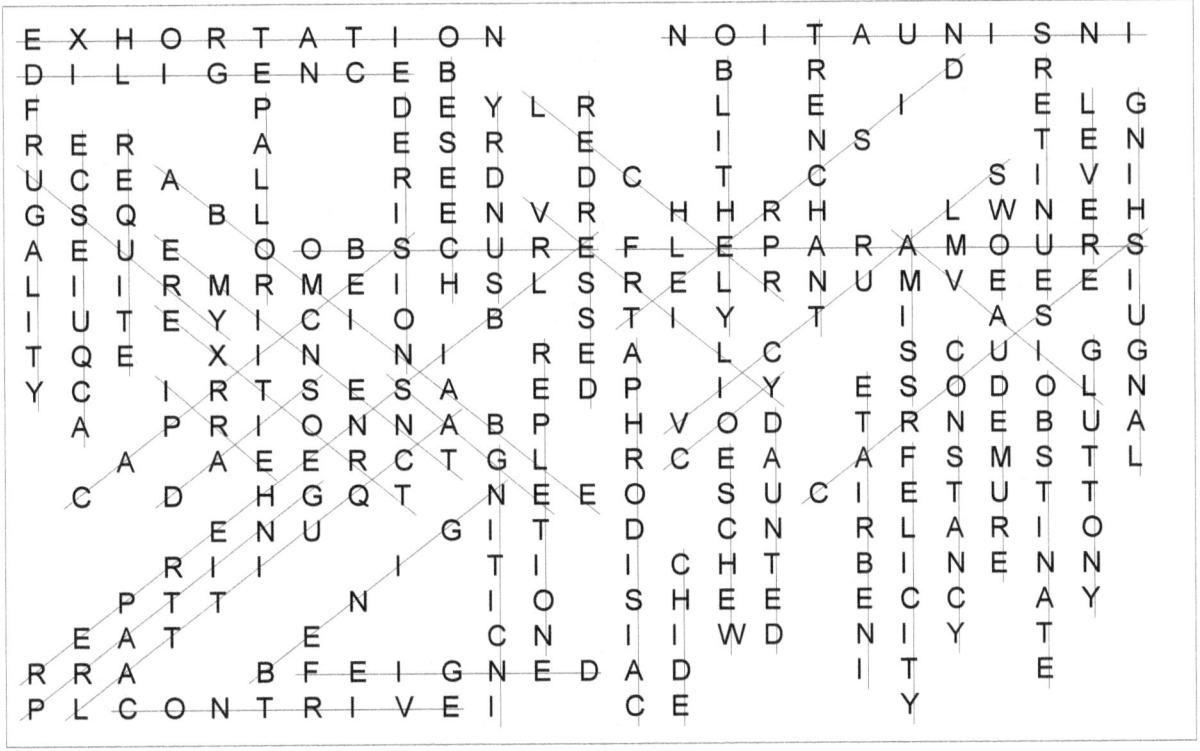

ABOMINABLE	DERISION	OBSTINATE
ACQUIESCE	DILIGENCE	PALLOR
ACQUITTAL	DISCREET	PARAMOURS
AMISS	EMINENT	PELF
APHRODISIAC	ESCHEW	PRATING
AVAIL	EXHORTATION	REDRESSED
BENIGN	EXTORT	REPLETION
BESEECH	FEIGNED	REPREHENSIBLE
BLITHELY	FELICITY	REQUITE
CAPRICES	FRUGALITY	RETINUE
CAROUSES	GLUTTONY	REVEL
CHIDE	INCITING	SAGE
CONSTANCY	INEBRIATE	SUNDRY
CONTRIVE	INSINUATION	TRENCHANT
COY	IRE	USURY
DAIS	LANGUISHING	VERILY
DAUNTED	LECHER	VICTUALS
DEMURE	OBSCURE	WOE

Canterbury Tales Vocabulary Crossword 1

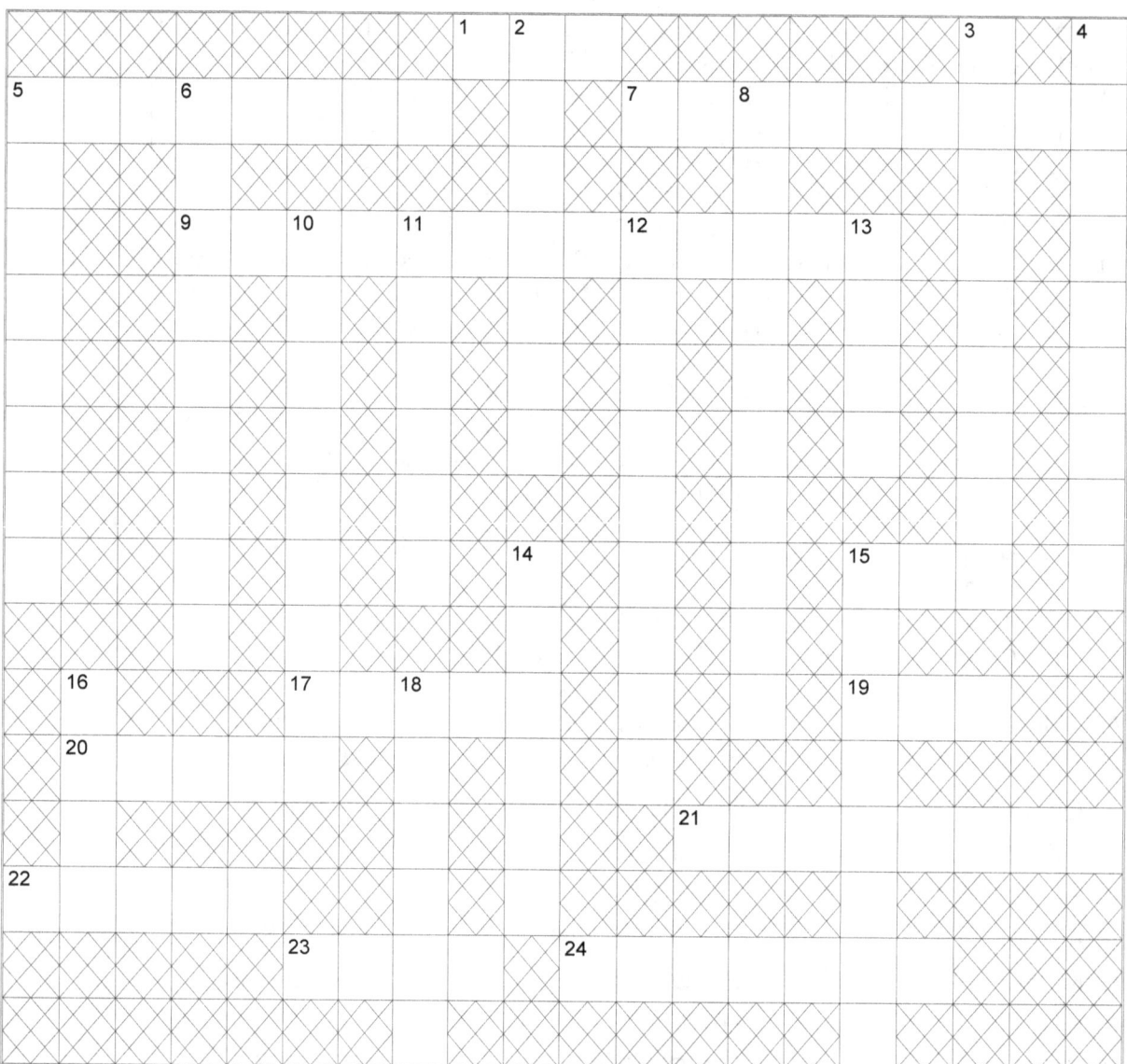

Across
1. A cause of suffering or harm
5. Behaves riotously; revels
7. Full to or beyond satisfaction
9. Appeals; pleas
15. Anger
17. To behave festively; frolic
19. Given to flirting
20. Wrong; awry
21. Lightheartedly; festively; merrily
22. Lending money & charging outrageously high interest
23. Loot; goods seized unlawfully
24. Widely known; famous

Down
2. Not readily noticed or seen; unknown
3. Steady attention and effort
4. Drunk
5. Whims
6. Stubborn
8. Of extraordinary size and/or power
10. Lovers
11. A man who overindulges in sexual activities
12. Sharp
13. Wise; wise person; scholarly
14. Extreme paleness
15. Stirring to action
16. A raised platform
18. Even; indeed

Canterbury Tales Vocabulary Crossword 1 Answer Key

							1 W	2 O	E				3 D		4 I
5 C	A	R	O	U	S	E	S		B		7 R	8 E	P	L	E	T	I	O	N

(Grid as shown)

Across
1. A cause of suffering or harm — **WOE**
5. Behaves riotously; revels — **CAROUSES**
7. Full to or beyond satisfaction — **REPLETION**
9. Appeals; pleas — **SUPPLICATIONS**
15. Anger — **IRE**
17. To behave festively; frolic — **REVEL**
19. Given to flirting — **COY**
20. Wrong; awry — **AMISS**
21. Lightheartedly; festively; merrily — **BLITHELY**
22. Lending money & charging outrageously high interest — **USURY**
23. Loot; goods seized unlawfully — **PELF**
24. Widely known; famous — **EMINENT**

Down
2. Not readily noticed or seen; unknown
3. Steady attention and effort
4. Drunk
5. Whims
6. Stubborn
8. Of extraordinary size and/or power
10. Lovers
11. A man who overindulges in sexual activities
12. Sharp
13. Wise; wise person; scholarly
14. Extreme paleness
15. Stirring to action
16. A raised platform
18. Even; indeed

Canterbury Tales Vocabulary Crossword 2

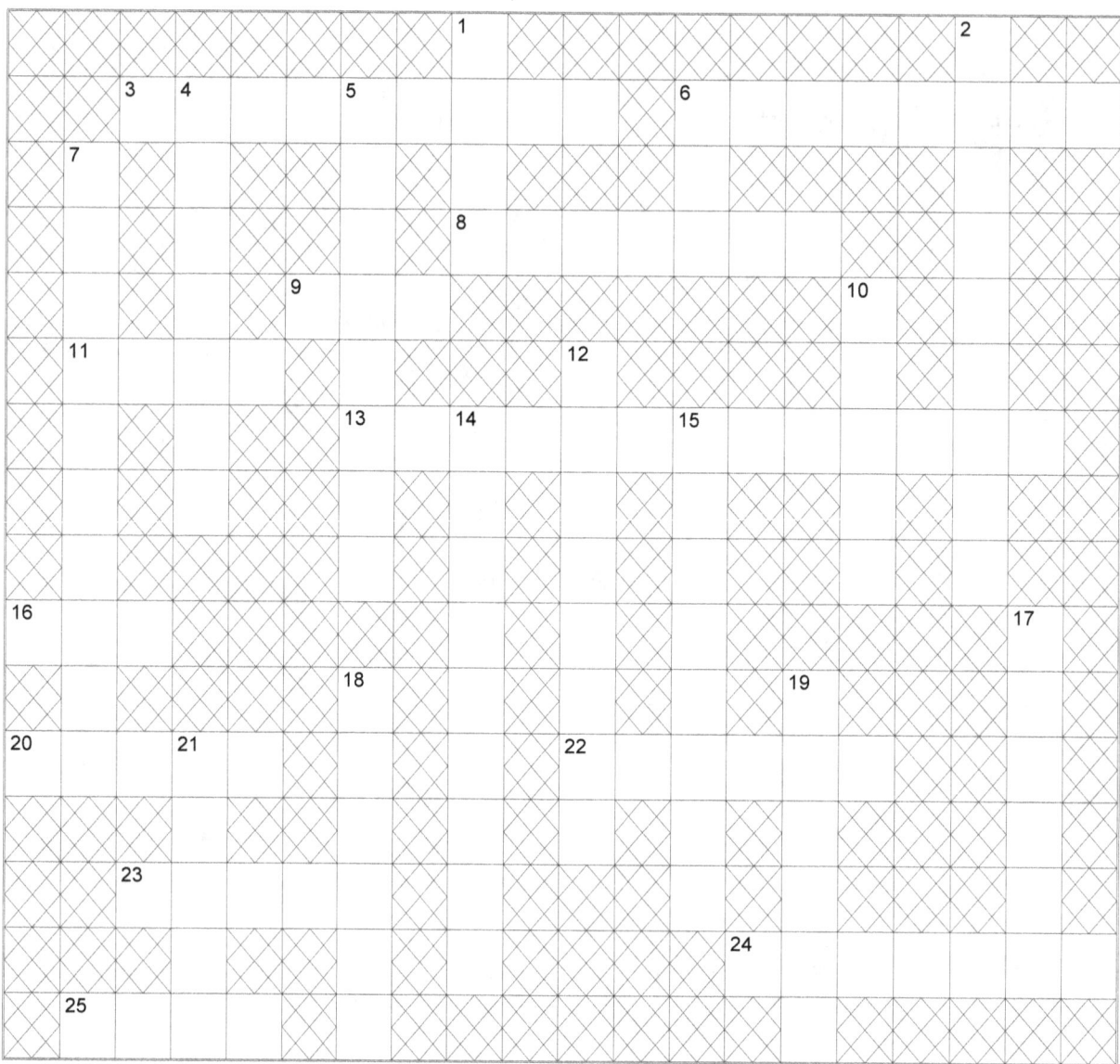

Across
3. Sharp
6. Stirring to action
8. Widely known; famous
9. A cause of suffering or harm
11. A raised platform
13. Appeals; pleas
16. Given to flirting
20. Lending money & charging outrageously high interest
22. A man who overindulges in sexual activities
23. Usefulness
24. Chattering; jabbering
25. Loot; goods seized unlawfully

Down
1. Wise; wise person; scholarly
2. Steady attention and effort
4. Repay
5. Behaves riotously; revels
6. Anger
7. Of extraordinary size and/or power
10. Wrong; awry
12. Lightheartedly; festively; merrily
14. Lovers
15. Whims
17. Kindhearted, considerate
18. Extreme paleness
19. Reserved in manner; shy; modest
21. To behave festively; frolic

Canterbury Tales Vocabulary Crossword 2 Answer Key

Across
3. Sharp
6. Stirring to action
8. Widely known; famous
9. A cause of suffering or harm
11. A raised platform
13. Appeals; pleas
16. Given to flirting
20. Lending money & charging outrageously high interest
22. A man who overindulges in sexual activities
23. Usefulness
24. Chattering; jabbering
25. Loot; goods seized unlawfully

Down
1. Wise; wise person; scholarly
2. Steady attention and effort
4. Repay
5. Behaves riotously; revels
6. Anger
7. Of extraordinary size and/or power
10. Wrong; awry
12. Lightheartedly; festively; merrily
14. Lovers
15. Whims
17. Kindhearted, considerate
18. Extreme paleness
19. Reserved in manner; shy; modest
21. To behave festively; frolic

Canterbury Tales Vocabulary Crossword 3

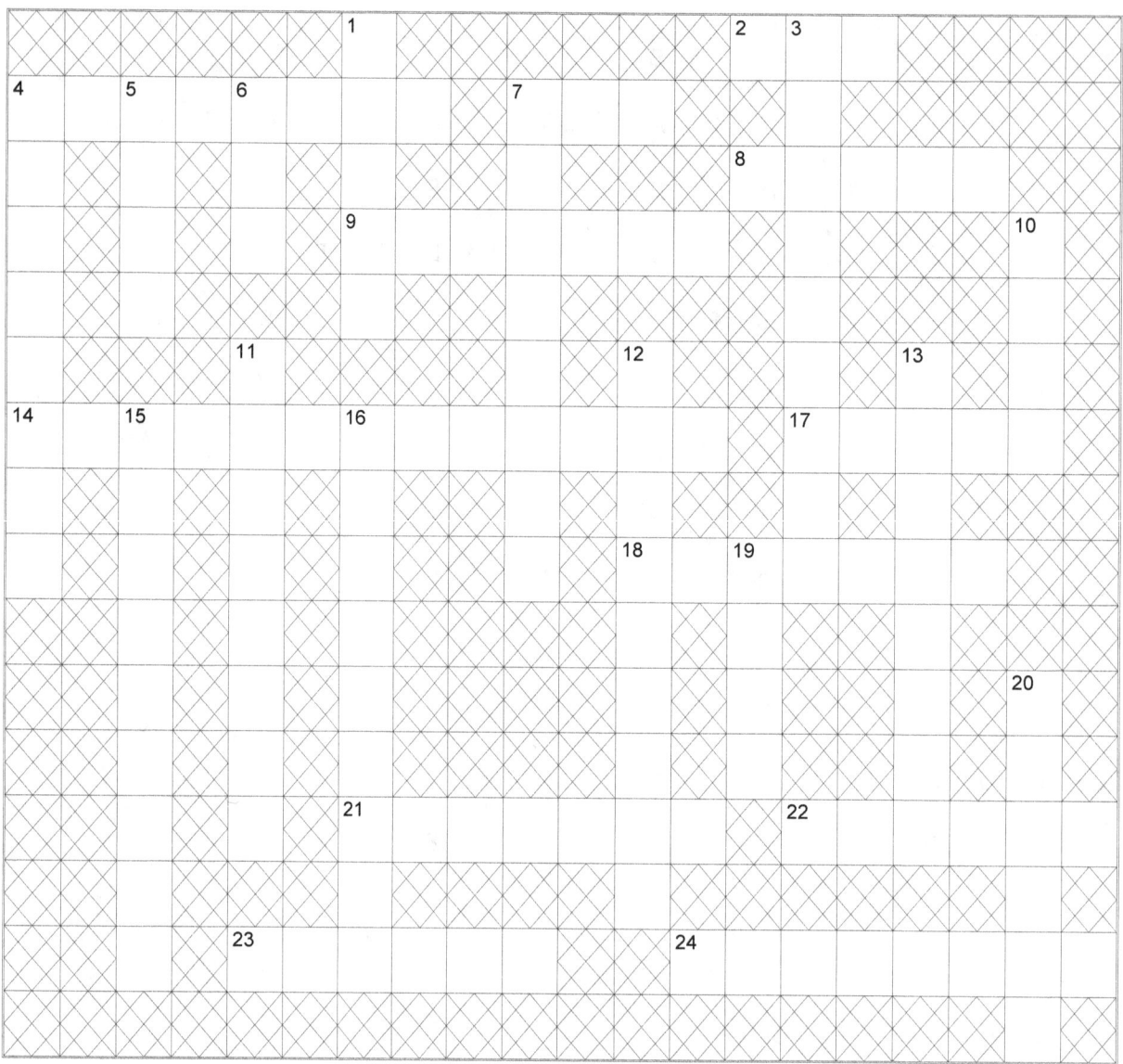

Across
2. A cause of suffering or harm
4. Whims
7. Given to flirting
8. Lending money & charging outrageously high interest
9. Widely known; famous
14. Appeals; pleas
17. Wrong; awry
18. Make an earnest request
21. Repay
22. To obtain from another by intimidation or blackmail
23. Reserved in manner; shy; modest
24. Food for humans

Down
1. To behave festively; frolic
3. Stubborn
4. Behaves riotously; revels
5. Loot; goods seized unlawfully
6. Anger
7. Plan
10. A raised platform
11. Lightheartedly; festively; merrily
12. Drunk
13. Diplomatic; politic; tactful
15. Lovers
16. A mystery; a puzzle
19. Wise; wise person; scholarly
20. Even; indeed

Canterbury Tales Vocabulary Crossword 3 Answer Key

Across
- 2. A cause of suffering or harm
- 4. Whims
- 7. Given to flirting
- 8. Lending money & charging outrageously high interest
- 9. Widely known; famous
- 14. Appeals; pleas
- 17. Wrong; awry
- 18. Make an earnest request
- 21. Repay
- 22. To obtain from another by intimidation or blackmail
- 23. Reserved in manner; shy; modest
- 24. Food for humans

Down
- 1. To behave festively; frolic
- 3. Stubborn
- 4. Behaves riotously; revels
- 5. Loot; goods seized unlawfully
- 6. Anger
- 7. Plan
- 10. A raised platform
- 11. Lightheartedly; festively; merrily
- 12. Drunk
- 13. Diplomatic; politic; tactful
- 15. Lovers
- 16. A mystery; a puzzle
- 19. Wise; wise person; scholarly
- 20. Even; indeed

Canterbury Tales Vocabulary Crossword 4

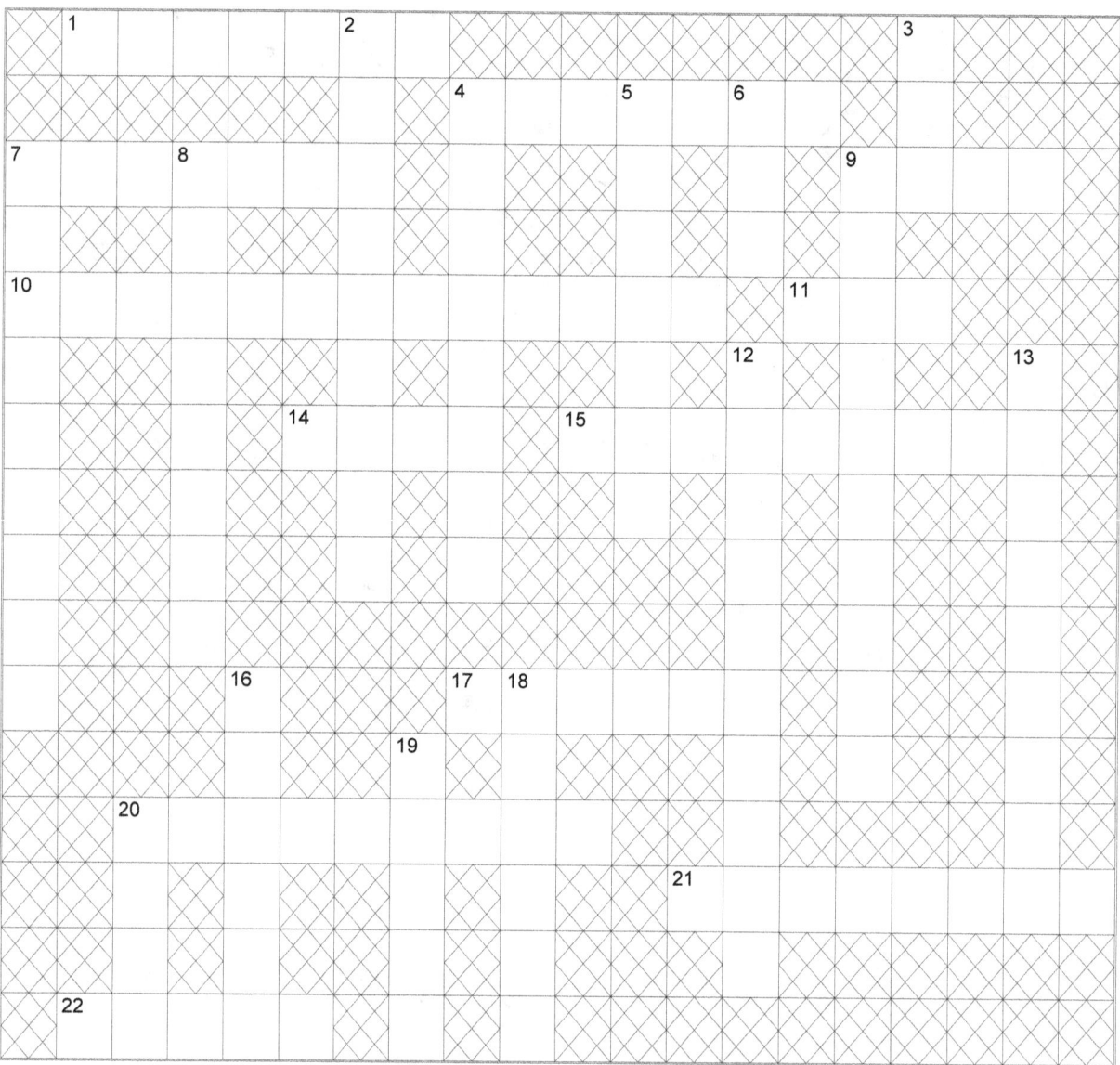

Across
1. Repay
4. Make an earnest request
7. Not readily noticed or seen; unknown
9. Loot; goods seized unlawfully
10. Appeals; pleas
11. A cause of suffering or harm
14. Wise; wise person; scholarly
15. Drunk
17. Kindhearted, considerate
20. Steady attention and effort
21. The vice of continually overeating
22. Lending money & charging outrageously high interest

Down
2. Sharp
3. Anger
4. Lightheartedly; festively; merrily
5. Widely known; famous
6. Given to flirting
7. Stubborn
8. Whims
9. Of extraordinary size and/or power
12. Hateful; horrid; awful
13. Full to or beyond satisfaction
16. Extreme paleness
18. To stay away from
19. To behave festively; frolic
20. A raised platform

Canterbury Tales Vocabulary Crossword 4 Answer Key

Across
1. Repay
4. Make an earnest request
7. Not readily noticed or seen; unknown
9. Loot; goods seized unlawfully
10. Appeals; pleas
11. A cause of suffering or harm
14. Wise; wise person; scholarly
15. Drunk
17. Kindhearted, considerate
20. Steady attention and effort
21. The vice of continually overeating
22. Lending money & charging outrageously high interest

Down
2. Sharp
3. Anger
4. Lightheartedly; festively; merrily
5. Widely known; famous
6. Given to flirting
7. Stubborn
8. Whims
9. Of extraordinary size and/or power
12. Hateful; horrid; awful
13. Full to or beyond satisfaction
16. Extreme paleness
18. To stay away from
19. To behave festively; frolic
20. A raised platform

Canterbury Tales Vocabulary Juggle Letters 1

1. SYRUU = 1. _____
   Lending money & charging outrageously high interest

2. VTICREON = 2. _____
   Plan

3. YELRIV = 3. _____
   Even; indeed

4. THNALLERDE = 4. _____
   Enchanted; fascinated

5. TNIGAPR = 5. _____
   Chattering; jabbering

6. AINIEETRB = 6. _____
   Drunk

7. PELF = 7. _____
   Loot; goods seized unlawfully

8. INEEGFD = 8. _____
   Artificial; counterfeited; faked

9. ESSDEDERR = 9. _____
   To get revenge for

10. DAIS =10. _____
    A raised platform

11. IPESCCRA =11. _____
    Whims

12. GLFURAYTI =12. _____
    Thriftiness; careful use of material goods

13. SUEAOCRS =13. _____
    Behaves riotously; revels

14. NASITBEOT =14. _____
    Stubborn

15. UOASMRAPR =15. _____
    Lovers

Canterbury Tales Vocabulary Juggle Letters 1 Answer Key

1. SYRUU = 1. USURY
   Lending money & charging outrageously high interest

2. VTICREON = 2. CONTRIVE
   Plan

3. YELRIV = 3. VERILY
   Even; indeed

4. THNALLERDE = 4. ENTHRALLED
   Enchanted; fascinated

5. TNIGAPR = 5. PRATING
   Chattering; jabbering

6. AINIEETRB = 6. INEBRIATE
   Drunk

7. PELF = 7. PELF
   Loot; goods seized unlawfully

8. INEEGFD = 8. FEIGNED
   Artificial; counterfeited; faked

9. ESSDEDERR = 9. REDRESSED
   To get revenge for

10. DAIS = 10. DAIS
    A raised platform

11. IPESCCRA = 11. CAPRICES
    Whims

12. GLFURAYTI = 12. FRUGALITY
    Thriftiness; careful use of material goods

13. SUEAOCRS = 13. CAROUSES
    Behaves riotously; revels

14. NASITBEOT = 14. OBSTINATE
    Stubborn

15. UOASMRAPR = 15. PARAMOURS
    Lovers

Canterbury Tales Vocabulary Juggle Letters 2

1. ERREDSDES = 1. _____
   To get revenge for

2. REI = 2. _____
   Anger

3. GNARTIP = 3. _____
   Chattering; jabbering

4. ASEG = 4. _____
   Wise; wise person; scholarly

5. LAPLOR = 5. _____
   Extreme paleness

6. NIHRAXEOTTO = 6. _____
   Speech that incites

7. ISMSA = 7. _____
   Wrong; awry

8. ETRQUEI = 8. _____
   Repay

9. NRPAOEIIDNESTT = 9. _____
   Belief that one's fate is already decided

10. YURSU =10. _____
    Lending money & charging outrageously high interest

11. EEUQHTBA =11. _____
    To leave material goods by will

12. DUYRSN =12. _____
    Consisting of many different kinds

13. ENITBAOST =13. _____
    Stubborn

14. RLEHEC =14. _____
    A man who overindulges in sexual activities

15. ECAHRNNTT =15. _____
    Sharp

Canterbury Tales Vocabulary Juggle Letters 2 Answer Key

1. ERREDSDES = 1. REDRESSED
   To get revenge for

2. REI = 2. IRE
   Anger

3. GNARTIP = 3. PRATING
   Chattering; jabbering

4. ASEG = 4. SAGE
   Wise; wise person; scholarly

5. LAPLOR = 5. PALLOR
   Extreme paleness

6. NIHRAXEOTTO = 6. EXHORTATION
   Speech that incites

7. ISMSA = 7. AMISS
   Wrong; awry

8. ETRQUEI = 8. REQUITE
   Repay

9. NRPAOEIIDNESTT = 9. PREDESTINATION
   Belief that one's fate is already decided

10. YURSU = 10. USURY
    Lending money & charging outrageously high interest

11. EEUQHTBA = 11. BEQUEATH
    To leave material goods by will

12. DUYRSN = 12. SUNDRY
    Consisting of many different kinds

13. ENITBAOST = 13. OBSTINATE
    Stubborn

14. RLEHEC = 14. LECHER
    A man who overindulges in sexual activities

15. ECAHRNNTT = 15. TRENCHANT
    Sharp

Canterbury Tales Vocabulary Juggle Letters 3

1. IDSA = 1. _____
A raised platform

2. COUREBS = 2. _____
Not readily noticed or seen; unknown

3. IEQRUET = 3. _____
Repay

4. CAUILTTQA = 4. _____
To free from a charge or accusation

5. ITEYHLBL = 5. _____
Lightheartedly; festively; merrily

6. TNHETCANR = 6. _____
Sharp

7. TNIMNEE = 7. _____
Widely known; famous

8. ARNTHETXOOI = 8. _____
Speech that incites

9. GSAE = 9. _____
Wise; wise person; scholarly

10. ORPAMSURA = 10. _____
Lovers

11. BEEATIINR = 11. _____
Drunk

12. IRYEVL = 12. _____
Even; indeed

13. EOW = 13. _____
A cause of suffering or harm

14. TDDAUNE = 14. _____
Deprived of courage as a result of fear, anxiety or disgust

15. CIEGDEINL = 15. _____
Steady attention and effort

Canterbury Tales Vocabulary Juggle Letters 3 Answer Key

1. IDSA = 1. DAIS
   A raised platform

2. COUREBS = 2. OBSCURE
   Not readily noticed or seen; unknown

3. IEQRUET = 3. REQUITE
   Repay

4. CAUILTTQA = 4. ACQUITTAL
   To free from a charge or accusation

5. ITEYHLBL = 5. BLITHELY
   Lightheartedly; festively; merrily

6. TNHETCANR = 6. TRENCHANT
   Sharp

7. TNIMNEE = 7. EMINENT
   Widely known; famous

8. ARNTHETXOOI = 8. EXHORTATION
   Speech that incites

9. GSAE = 9. SAGE
   Wise; wise person; scholarly

10. ORPAMSURA =10. PARAMOURS
    Lovers

11. BEEATIINR =11. INEBRIATE
    Drunk

12. IRYEVL =12. VERILY
    Even; indeed

13. EOW =13. WOE
    A cause of suffering or harm

14. TDDAUNE =14. DAUNTED
    Deprived of courage as a result of fear, anxiety or disgust

15. CIEGDEINL =15. DILIGENCE
    Steady attention and effort

Canterbury Tales Vocabulary Juggle Letters 4

1. ARAPOUMSR = 1. _____
Lovers

2. NNBGEI = 2. _____
Kindhearted, considerate

3. REELV = 3. _____
To behave festively; frolic

4. OSCRASEU = 4. _____
Behaves riotously; revels

5. HSREELINREEPB = 5. _____
Deserving condemnation; despicable

6. XTTROE = 6. _____
To obtain from another by intimidation or blackmail

7. GANRIPT = 7. _____
Chattering; jabbering

8. AUIRGTFLY = 8. _____
Thriftiness; careful use of material goods

9. YSUUR = 9. _____
Lending money & charging outrageously high interest

10. ARSPNTITIDEOEN =10. _____
Belief that one's fate is already decided

11. EELNHTALDR =11. _____
Enchanted; fascinated

12. UQEHTBAE =12. _____
To leave material goods by will

13. ESAG =13. _____
Wise; wise person; scholarly

14. LIEPRETON =14. _____
Full to or beyond satisfaction

15. UNRNDOCUM =15. _____
A mystery; a puzzle

Canterbury Tales Vocabulary Juggle Letters 4 Answer Key

1. ARAPOUMSR = 1. PARAMOURS
Lovers

2. NNBGEI = 2. BENIGN
Kindhearted, considerate

3. REELV = 3. REVEL
To behave festively; frolic

4. OSCRASEU = 4. CAROUSES
Behaves riotously; revels

5. HSREELINREEPB = 5. REPREHENSIBLE
Deserving condemnation; despicable

6. XTTROE = 6. EXTORT
To obtain from another by intimidation or blackmail

7. GANRIPT = 7. PRATING
Chattering; jabbering

8. AUIRGTFLY = 8. FRUGALITY
Thriftiness; careful use of material goods

9. YSUUR = 9. USURY
Lending money & charging outrageously high interest

10. ARSPNTITIDEOEN =10. PREDESTINATION
Belief that one's fate is already decided

11. EELNHTALDR =11. ENTHRALLED
Enchanted; fascinated

12. UQEHTBAE =12. BEQUEATH
To leave material goods by will

13. ESAG =13. SAGE
Wise; wise person; scholarly

14. LIEPRETON =14. REPLETION
Full to or beyond satisfaction

15. UNRNDOCUM =15. CONUNDRUM
A mystery; a puzzle

ABOMINABLE	Hateful; horrid; awful
ACQUIESCE	Agree; consent
ACQUITTAL	To free from a charge or accusation
AMISS	Wrong; awry
APHRODISIAC	A drug or food having the effect of arousing sexual desire
AVAIL	Usefulness

BENIGN	Kindhearted, considerate
BEQUEATH	To leave material goods by will
BESEECH	Make an earnest request
BLITHELY	Lightheartedly; festively; merrily
CAPRICES	Whims
CAROUSES	Behaves riotously; revels

CHIDE	To criticize for a fault or offense
CONSTANCY	Faithfulness; fidelity
CONTRIVE	Plan
CONUNDRUM	A mystery; a puzzle
COY	Given to flirting
DAIS	A raised platform

DAUNTED	Deprived of courage as a result of fear, anxiety or disgust
DEMURE	Reserved in manner; shy; modest
DERISION	Mockery; ridicule
DILIGENCE	Steady attention and effort
DISCREET	Diplomatic; politic; tactful
EMINENT	Widely known; famous

ENTHRALLED	Enchanted; fascinated
ESCHEW	To stay away from
EXHORTATION	Speech that incites
EXTORT	To obtain from another by intimidation or blackmail
FEIGNED	Artificial; counterfeited; faked
FELICITY	Happiness; bliss

FRUGALITY	Thriftiness; careful use of material goods
GLUTTONY	The vice of continually overeating
INCITING	Stirring to action
INEBRIATE	Drunk
INSINUATION	Innuendoes; indirect hints; implications
IRE	Anger

LANGUISHING	Lacking energy or strength
LECHER	A man who overindulges in sexual activities
OBSCURE	Not readily noticed or seen; unknown
OBSTINATE	Stubborn
PALLOR	Extreme paleness
PARAMOURS	Lovers

PELF	Loot; goods seized unlawfully
PRATING	Chattering; jabbering
PREDESTINATION	Belief that one's fate is already decided
PREROGATIVE	The right to command or decide
PRODIGIOUS	Of extraordinary size and/or power
PROFFERING	To put before another for acceptance

REDRESSED	To get revenge for
REPLETION	Full to or beyond satisfaction
REPREHENSIBLE	Deserving condemnation; despicable
REQUITE	Repay
RETINUE	Group of attendants or followers
REVEL	To behave festively; frolic

SAGE	Wise; wise person; scholarly
SUNDRY	Consisting of many different kinds
SUPPLICATIONS	Appeals; pleas
TRENCHANT	Sharp
USURY	Lending money & charging outrageously high interest
VERILY	Even; indeed

VICTUALS	Food for humans
WOE	A cause of suffering or harm

Canterbury Tales Vocabulary

OBSTINATE	FRUGALITY	INSINUATION	AVAIL	INEBRIATE
LECHER	REQUITE	DILIGENCE	SUPPLICATIONS	EMINENT
COY	CONTRIVE	FREE SPACE	INCITING	GLUTTONY
SAGE	PALLOR	BEQUEATH	ENTHRALLED	PROFFERING
PARAMOURS	BLITHELY	DEMURE	WOE	EXHORTATION

Canterbury Tales Vocabulary

LANGUISHING	FEIGNED	PRATING	REVEL	CONUNDRUM
REPLETION	PREROGATIVE	IRE	VERILY	BESEECH
SUNDRY	AMISS	FREE SPACE	CONSTANCY	BENIGN
ABOMINABLE	DAUNTED	DERISION	APHRODISIAC	DAIS
EXTORT	REPREHENSIBLE	DISCREET	ACQUITTAL	ACQUIESCE

Canterbury Tales Vocabulary

DILIGENCE	COY	SUNDRY	DAUNTED	GLUTTONY
BESEECH	CHIDE	INCITING	PREDESTINATION	IRE
INSINUATION	AVAIL	FREE SPACE	OBSTINATE	CONUNDRUM
LECHER	CONSTANCY	DAIS	ACQUIESCE	EMINENT
VICTUALS	PALLOR	OBSCURE	EXHORTATION	FEIGNED

Canterbury Tales Vocabulary

REQUITE	REVEL	FELICITY	USURY	AMISS
APHRODISIAC	INEBRIATE	SAGE	ENTHRALLED	SUPPLICATIONS
PRATING	ACQUITTAL	FREE SPACE	ESCHEW	TRENCHANT
ABOMINABLE	EXTORT	DERISION	BEQUEATH	FRUGALITY
BENIGN	REDRESSED	PROFFERING	PARAMOURS	PRODIGIOUS

Canterbury Tales Vocabulary

EXHORTATION	TRENCHANT	RETINUE	REQUITE	DAUNTED
IRE	COY	REPLETION	APHRODISIAC	AMISS
PREDESTINATION	BLITHELY	FREE SPACE	EXTORT	BENIGN
DERISION	USURY	VERILY	LECHER	PALLOR
CHIDE	EMINENT	AVAIL	PRATING	INEBRIATE

Canterbury Tales Vocabulary

INSINUATION	SUNDRY	LANGUISHING	DEMURE	BESEECH
CAROUSES	INCITING	ACQUIESCE	DAIS	CONUNDRUM
ABOMINABLE	FELICITY	FREE SPACE	SUPPLICATIONS	FEIGNED
ESCHEW	OBSTINATE	CONTRIVE	VICTUALS	WOE
REVEL	REPREHENSIBLE	PREROGATIVE	CAPRICES	BEQUEATH

Canterbury Tales Vocabulary

PREROGATIVE	AMISS	INEBRIATE	ESCHEW	DILIGENCE
ACQUIESCE	REDRESSED	REQUITE	AVAIL	CAPRICES
PRODIGIOUS	RETINUE	FREE SPACE	BLITHELY	BESEECH
PREDESTINATION	PALLOR	EXTORT	CONUNDRUM	CONTRIVE
OBSTINATE	DISCREET	WOE	BEQUEATH	GLUTTONY

Canterbury Tales Vocabulary

REVEL	BENIGN	CONSTANCY	PROFFERING	VICTUALS
DERISION	ABOMINABLE	CAROUSES	EXHORTATION	COY
VERILY	PRATING	FREE SPACE	SUNDRY	TRENCHANT
DEMURE	DAIS	ACQUITTAL	SUPPLICATIONS	REPREHENSIBLE
OBSCURE	REPLETION	USURY	SAGE	IRE

Canterbury Tales Vocabulary

SUNDRY	INCITING	EXHORTATION	RETINUE	BEQUEATH
DAIS	FRUGALITY	DISCREET	INEBRIATE	REPREHENSIBLE
REQUITE	LECHER	FREE SPACE	AVAIL	REPLETION
PREROGATIVE	ACQUITTAL	BLITHELY	WOE	ESCHEW
PELF	PROFFERING	CAROUSES	FELICITY	ACQUIESCE

Canterbury Tales Vocabulary

ENTHRALLED	BENIGN	SAGE	PARAMOURS	CHIDE
CONSTANCY	EXTORT	PALLOR	FEIGNED	EMINENT
VERILY	CAPRICES	FREE SPACE	PREDESTINATION	LANGUISHING
OBSCURE	REDRESSED	DERISION	AMISS	CONUNDRUM
DEMURE	USURY	IRE	SUPPLICATIONS	APHRODISIAC

Canterbury Tales Vocabulary

EXTORT	CONSTANCY	ABOMINABLE	APHRODISIAC	PRODIGIOUS
FELICITY	PARAMOURS	BENIGN	CHIDE	LECHER
VICTUALS	DILIGENCE	FREE SPACE	INEBRIATE	LANGUISHING
AVAIL	AMISS	COY	PELF	PROFFERING
CONTRIVE	DEMURE	OBSCURE	DAUNTED	WOE

Canterbury Tales Vocabulary

FEIGNED	RETINUE	IRE	GLUTTONY	CONUNDRUM
INCITING	ACQUITTAL	BESEECH	FRUGALITY	USURY
REQUITE	REDRESSED	FREE SPACE	EMINENT	CAPRICES
DAIS	PREDESTINATION	OBSTINATE	INSINUATION	BLITHELY
SAGE	REPLETION	PALLOR	ENTHRALLED	DISCREET

Canterbury Tales Vocabulary

DERISION	ABOMINABLE	PRODIGIOUS	REDRESSED	USURY
BESEECH	ENTHRALLED	REQUITE	SUNDRY	GLUTTONY
INCITING	PELF	FREE SPACE	LECHER	INEBRIATE
BLITHELY	PREROGATIVE	CONUNDRUM	BENIGN	EXTORT
DAUNTED	DISCREET	PROFFERING	PREDESTINATION	CHIDE

Canterbury Tales Vocabulary

CAROUSES	EXHORTATION	DILIGENCE	OBSCURE	FEIGNED
PALLOR	CONTRIVE	BEQUEATH	SUPPLICATIONS	REVEL
FRUGALITY	FELICITY	FREE SPACE	INSINUATION	AVAIL
VERILY	CONSTANCY	IRE	SAGE	DEMURE
LANGUISHING	EMINENT	REPREHENSIBLE	ACQUIESCE	OBSTINATE

Canterbury Tales Vocabulary

AMISS	INSINUATION	FELICITY	CONUNDRUM	INEBRIATE
CONSTANCY	OBSCURE	PREROGATIVE	RETINUE	PELF
COY	DAIS	FREE SPACE	REPLETION	APHRODISIAC
EXTORT	DISCREET	PARAMOURS	INCITING	VICTUALS
PROFFERING	REQUITE	BESEECH	FRUGALITY	DERISION

Canterbury Tales Vocabulary

REPREHENSIBLE	FEIGNED	EMINENT	EXHORTATION	TRENCHANT
PREDESTINATION	ACQUIESCE	SUNDRY	SAGE	BEQUEATH
ACQUITTAL	REDRESSED	FREE SPACE	LECHER	BENIGN
PRATING	USURY	LANGUISHING	ABOMINABLE	SUPPLICATIONS
IRE	CHIDE	REVEL	DEMURE	ESCHEW

Canterbury Tales Vocabulary

INSINUATION	PELF	GLUTTONY	RETINUE	BLITHELY
CHIDE	SAGE	PRODIGIOUS	FEIGNED	AVAIL
PREROGATIVE	VICTUALS	FREE SPACE	PRATING	REPREHENSIBLE
SUPPLICATIONS	USURY	DAUNTED	INCITING	EXHORTATION
EXTORT	PREDESTINATION	BEQUEATH	SUNDRY	CAROUSES

Canterbury Tales Vocabulary

DILIGENCE	CONTRIVE	ABOMINABLE	ACQUITTAL	CONSTANCY
OBSTINATE	CONUNDRUM	REPLETION	LANGUISHING	ENTHRALLED
TRENCHANT	ESCHEW	FREE SPACE	LECHER	REVEL
BESEECH	REQUITE	BENIGN	COY	PALLOR
CAPRICES	EMINENT	DERISION	AMISS	VERILY

Canterbury Tales Vocabulary

PALLOR	APHRODISIAC	CONTRIVE	OBSCURE	PRODIGIOUS
AVAIL	LANGUISHING	ESCHEW	GLUTTONY	EMINENT
PREDESTINATION	DEMURE	FREE SPACE	VERILY	BEQUEATH
WOE	IRE	DILIGENCE	SUPPLICATIONS	ENTHRALLED
CAROUSES	CONUNDRUM	ACQUIESCE	FEIGNED	REQUITE

Canterbury Tales Vocabulary

PROFFERING	BLITHELY	DAIS	FELICITY	ABOMINABLE
CAPRICES	INCITING	CONSTANCY	PREROGATIVE	REPREHENSIBLE
PARAMOURS	LECHER	FREE SPACE	INEBRIATE	PRATING
REDRESSED	REPLETION	EXHORTATION	USURY	DAUNTED
INSINUATION	EXTORT	OBSTINATE	AMISS	PELF

Canterbury Tales Vocabulary

CAROUSES	PELF	DERISION	RETINUE	TRENCHANT
BLITHELY	USURY	FEIGNED	APHRODISIAC	REPREHENSIBLE
AMISS	PREDESTINATION	FREE SPACE	ESCHEW	PREROGATIVE
INSINUATION	INCITING	CHIDE	EMINENT	PRODIGIOUS
REQUITE	REVEL	ENTHRALLED	EXTORT	SAGE

Canterbury Tales Vocabulary

OBSCURE	VERILY	BEQUEATH	CONTRIVE	BESEECH
AVAIL	IRE	COY	WOE	DEMURE
DAUNTED	INEBRIATE	FREE SPACE	DISCREET	ACQUITTAL
SUPPLICATIONS	ABOMINABLE	FRUGALITY	OBSTINATE	PALLOR
PRATING	REPLETION	LANGUISHING	DAIS	ACQUIESCE

Canterbury Tales Vocabulary

VICTUALS	DAUNTED	RETINUE	USURY	PREROGATIVE
ENTHRALLED	SUNDRY	INSINUATION	DAIS	SAGE
REQUITE	AVAIL	FREE SPACE	DISCREET	TRENCHANT
CONSTANCY	FEIGNED	PELF	LANGUISHING	INEBRIATE
CAROUSES	ESCHEW	PRODIGIOUS	OBSCURE	GLUTTONY

Canterbury Tales Vocabulary

REPLETION	AMISS	APHRODISIAC	FRUGALITY	ABOMINABLE
ACQUIESCE	CONTRIVE	INCITING	PRATING	PALLOR
DERISION	FELICITY	FREE SPACE	REVEL	DILIGENCE
BLITHELY	WOE	CONUNDRUM	EXHORTATION	COY
SUPPLICATIONS	PREDESTINATION	CAPRICES	IRE	LECHER

Canterbury Tales Vocabulary

BLITHELY	EMINENT	VERILY	DERISION	REPREHENSIBLE
USURY	DISCREET	CONTRIVE	CAPRICES	WOE
BEQUEATH	SUPPLICATIONS	FREE SPACE	REPLETION	ENTHRALLED
BENIGN	BESEECH	REVEL	ACQUIESCE	OBSTINATE
INEBRIATE	EXHORTATION	AMISS	CONSTANCY	FELICITY

Canterbury Tales Vocabulary

PRATING	INCITING	IRE	SAGE	DEMURE
REQUITE	REDRESSED	PREROGATIVE	OBSCURE	CAROUSES
LECHER	RETINUE	FREE SPACE	VICTUALS	GLUTTONY
COY	LANGUISHING	PREDESTINATION	INSINUATION	ABOMINABLE
APHRODISIAC	FRUGALITY	PALLOR	DILIGENCE	AVAIL

Canterbury Tales Vocabulary

SAGE	REQUITE	EXTORT	INEBRIATE	LECHER
DISCREET	PRATING	ACQUIESCE	GLUTTONY	ESCHEW
AVAIL	ABOMINABLE	FREE SPACE	DEMURE	VICTUALS
EXHORTATION	OBSCURE	AMISS	DAIS	BEQUEATH
CONUNDRUM	DERISION	CAPRICES	ACQUITTAL	ENTHRALLED

Canterbury Tales Vocabulary

DAUNTED	REPREHENSIBLE	REVEL	PARAMOURS	FRUGALITY
PELF	USURY	WOE	APHRODISIAC	DILIGENCE
INSINUATION	PREROGATIVE	FREE SPACE	COY	RETINUE
FELICITY	BLITHELY	OBSTINATE	INCITING	LANGUISHING
REDRESSED	PREDESTINATION	VERILY	SUNDRY	REPLETION

Canterbury Tales Vocabulary

EXTORT	OBSCURE	REVEL	PRATING	ESCHEW
CAPRICES	ACQUIESCE	AVAIL	LECHER	VERILY
IRE	ACQUITTAL	FREE SPACE	USURY	DERISION
REPLETION	DAIS	AMISS	SUPPLICATIONS	BESEECH
BEQUEATH	INSINUATION	REDRESSED	CONSTANCY	RETINUE

Canterbury Tales Vocabulary

BENIGN	CHIDE	CONUNDRUM	WOE	BLITHELY
DAUNTED	DISCREET	PARAMOURS	DILIGENCE	CAROUSES
CONTRIVE	ABOMINABLE	FREE SPACE	REPREHENSIBLE	EXHORTATION
COY	INEBRIATE	OBSTINATE	SUNDRY	FELICITY
FRUGALITY	PRODIGIOUS	ENTHRALLED	PALLOR	PELF

Canterbury Tales Vocabulary

PARAMOURS	VERILY	RETINUE	INCITING	REQUITE
ACQUITTAL	ABOMINABLE	APHRODISIAC	SAGE	IRE
BESEECH	TRENCHANT	FREE SPACE	PRATING	PREROGATIVE
BEQUEATH	REPLETION	REDRESSED	EXHORTATION	GLUTTONY
USURY	SUNDRY	CAROUSES	LECHER	ENTHRALLED

Canterbury Tales Vocabulary

REPREHENSIBLE	CHIDE	PROFFERING	AMISS	CONUNDRUM
FELICITY	EMINENT	EXTORT	BLITHELY	SUPPLICATIONS
OBSTINATE	DEMURE	FREE SPACE	COY	FEIGNED
ACQUIESCE	FRUGALITY	PELF	PALLOR	CONTRIVE
PREDESTINATION	CONSTANCY	REVEL	CAPRICES	DISCREET